TRIUMPH SPORTS CARS

FROM THE 1930s TO THE 1980s

KEVIN WARRINGTON

AMBERLEY

About the Author

Kevin Warrington has a long family connection with what is loosely called 'the motor trade', reaching back to the origins of mechanised road transport, but chose a career in the computer industry until redundancy in 2001 allowed him to indulge a passion for writing, photography and classic machinery in general.

With his wife, Ann, he ran a specialist motor coach company for several years, operating a fleet of 1950s classic coaches used primarily for TV productions and film work as well as for wedding hire. He is the author of several books, all on the theme of classic vehicles, mostly with a strong connection to the Standard and Triumph marques.

He has been an occasional contributor of words and pictures to several classic transport magazines and formerly edited two Triumph club magazines: *TR Action* for the TR Register and *SIXappeal* for the Triumph 2000/2500/2.5 Register.

First published 2026

Amberley Publishing
The Hill, Stroud,
Gloucestershire, GL5 4EP

www.amberley-books.com

ISBN: 978 1 3981 3086 9 (print)
ISBN: 978 1 3981 3087 6 (ebook)

British Library Cataloguing in Publication Data.
A catalogue record for this book is available from the British Library.

Typeset in 10pt on 13pt Celeste.
Typesetting by SJmagic DESIGN SERVICES, India.
Printed in the UK.

Appointed GPSR EU Representative: Easy Access System Europe Oü, 16879218
Address: Mustamäe tee 50, 10621, Tallinn, Estonia
Contact Details: gpsr.requests@easproject.com, +358 40 500 3575

Contents

Introduction

What exactly is a sports car? A simple definition could be that it has high performance, gives an exhilarating ride, is probably an open-top or convertible car, but could also be a fastback or coupé style and has the credentials to participate in organised motor sport. Often, it will have just two seats, but some may have additional rear seating that is sometimes only comfortable for small children or for the shortest of journeys. It could also be extended to include Grand Touring cars that comprise sporting lines with a high power-to-weight ratio and capable of completing substantial distance in a single journey with the driver and passenger being transported in a stress-free, comfortable environment. In this book, we take the definition of a sports car as written above but also include the Triumph Stag, with its high power and creature comforts, as a good example of a Grand Touring car.

Triumph – The Very Beginning

Since the Triumph company's first entry into the car business in 1921 with the acquisition of the Dawson Car Company, the ambition to create cars with sporting attributes must have been apparent to capitalise on the success that the company had already achieved with its motorcycle products, which had been ridden to great success in many events, not least the Isle of Man TT, and had sold in large numbers, especially to the military during the First World War. New models followed and with well-known competition driver Donald Healey becoming a member of the management team, the focus on vehicles that met the definition of a sports car rapidly became clear.

However, the Triumph company continually struggled from one near financial disaster to another. To generate income, the motorcycle business was sold off and, after passing through various acquisitions, continues to produce highly regarded performance bikes to this day. In the late 1930s, the cash sums that had been invested in new models overwhelmed the company's ability to generate revenue and its bankers, then owed in excess of £150,000 (approximately £8,500,000 in 2025 value), called in Receivers. Donald Healey, still employed by the company, was involved in the search for a new owner, resulting in the company being sold as a going concern to the Sheffield-based industrial group of Thomas Ward & Company.

Early Triumph car models were simple, box-like affairs, in common with most of their competitors.

During the Second World War, the company, along with almost every engineering concern, was engaged on armaments work. Triumph was to suffer terminally during the Blitz, which resulted in the destruction of both the Coventry premises and machine tools of the company. Despite the efforts of Healey to convince Thomas Ward & Co. to continue building Triumph cars, the latter company decided to cut its losses and attempt to find a buyer for whatever could be salvaged of the Triumph company.

By the end of the 1930s, Triumph's models had developed a style all of their own, demonstrated to good effect by this pre-war Dolomite.

Standard Motor Company to the Rescue

At this point in the story, a saviour was found in the form of Sir John Black, then General Manager of the Standard Motor Company. Black had ambitions for Standard to develop a range of overtly sporting cars to compete with the likes of Jaguar, recently renamed from SS-Cars and Morgan. The availability of Triumph, even if it was just the brand name and goodwill, was attractive and a deal was quickly struck. Henceforth, Triumph cars would be built by Standard and the combined business would be known as Standard-Triumph. Remarkably, Sir John, then known as Captain John Black following his service in the Royal Tank Regiment during the First World War, had at one time been a director of Triumph while Seigfried Bettmann, founder of Triumph, had at one time held the office of chairman at Standard.

It was therefore from the late 1940s onwards that the Triumph name would grace a range of motor cars that were commercially successful, highly innovative and achieved significant competition success until the end of Triumph as a brand following a corporate reorganisation in the latter stages of the British Leyland empire. With the demise of British Leyland, the remaining brands went through a number of owners, including British Aerospace and BMW. When BMW disposed of their ownership, it is interesting to note that Triumph was one of two brand names that they chose to retain, the other being Riley, giving rise to hopes by enthusiasts that perhaps the famous Triumph name might one day return to the roads.

1

Pre-War Triumph Sports Cars

Triumph's early cars were traditional, box-styled affairs in keeping with the typical designs of the 1920s. The year 1927 saw the introduction of the Triumph Super Seven model range, including a two-seater convertible coupé, although two additional passengers could be carried using the 'dickey' or rumble seat that opened out from the boot space and provided rudimentary accommodation. The coupé was described in sales materials as being the car for 'the man who motors for the sake of motoring'. Sporting achievement was very much the domain of enthusiastic amateurs rather than factory sponsorship, with an early highlight being achieved in 1929 when Donald Healey drove through appalling weather to finish the Monte-Carlo Rally but was unfortunately outside of his designated time. He was to have better luck in 1930 when he finished in seventh place overall, and in 1931 when he won the event, but in that year his car of choice was an Invicta.

Triumph Appoint an Experimental Manager

In 1933, Healey joined the Triumph Company as Experimental Manager and in the same year, the Super Seven was replaced by the Super Eight. The new Eight model was more luxuriously trimmed than its predecessor but used the same engine – Triumph perhaps now accepted that the engine was actually rated at 8hp for taxation reasons.

A six-cylinder-powered model followed in quick succession and was given the name Scorpion. In the early 1930s, synchromesh gearboxes were not common, and many drivers struggling with the art of double declutching for downward gear changes were apt to hold a gear for as long as possible. Hence, an engine producing a high torque was an advantage – at least in those cars not fitted with the Wilson epicyclic pre-select gearbox. For many years the British road tax system was based on a nominal horsepower rating, which itself was calculated on total piston surface area, and within this format there was a period when it was possible to produce six-cylinder engines of relatively small displacement with just a small increase in road tax payable. But perhaps the 'hungry 1930s' was not the ideal time for such developments to be introduced.

By 1933, motorists had discovered that the gradual introduction of synchromesh, especially on the higher gears, coupled with more compliant engine mounts, negated the six-cylinder advantage of smoothness over the four. This then brought to an end the short fashion of relatively small-capacity six-cylinder engines. Selling only in small numbers, the Scorpion was soon re-equipped with a four-cylinder engine built by Triumph under licence from Coventry Climax, as the Super Nine and Super Ten saloon models, and when fitted with a two-seat sports-car-style body was named the Southern Cross.

Triumph Gloria

The autumn of 1933 also brought the introduction of an additional Triumph model range that has often been said to be the most stylish of all late pre-war British cars – the Triumph Gloria. Styled by Triumph's in-house designer, Frank Warner, the Gloria broke away from Triumph's previous benchmark of producing small, upright cars and instead, as Triumph's General Manager at the time, Claude Holbrook commented on its launch: '[It was] modern in conception, revealing lines of distinction that have never before been achieved.'

It was indeed a stylish design, often compared favourably to market-defining cars from the likes of Alvis and Riley. In common with Triumph's usual practice, the engines were built under licence from Coventry-Climax with raw castings being delivered to Triumph before machining and assembling. Under the influence of Donald Healey, the Gloria tourer was adapted into the Monte-Carlo version – clearly intended to those customers who might be interested in rallying. This model was easily identified by severely cutaway doors

Above and opposite above: Two examples of Triumph's Gloria Roadsters. Of note is the deep cutaway of the doors.

Above and overleaf above: Two images of a 1934 Gloria 'Monte Carlo', meticulously restored to original condition. Note again the deeply cutaway doors with filler panels inserted to accommodate wet weather side screens.

In common with most cars of the era, instrumentation is rudimentary with the speedometer and rev counter mounted centrally.

and twin spare wheels mounted onto the rear of the bodywork. The engine of 1,287cc capacity, fuelled by twin Zenith carburettors, produced 48bhp and the suspension of the car being quite conventional with leaf springs on each corner. For the 1934 Monte-Carlo Rally, Triumph entered a team of seven cars, but as none of the new Monte-Carlo models were actually available at the time, the engine was installed into two 10hp Southern Cross chassis sporting much modified bodywork, with the other five entrants being a mix of saloons and tourers. All seven Triumphs were to finish the event, collecting a plethora of silverware, with Healey finishing third overall and winner of his class.

An Early Grand Touring Model

Triumph's business was never likely to challenge the likes of Austin or Ford in terms of volume and therefore focussed on producing more upmarket models than its obvious competitors. It had been fortunate to have had Walter Belgrove as stylist, who years later was to have a profound input on the design of Triumph's post-war sports cars.

Above and right: Classic art deco design, this Gloria 'Free-Flow' shows the skill of designer Walter Belgrove to perfection.

The year 1935 saw the announcement of a six-cylinder-powered Gloria, which featured an aerodynamic body styled by Walter Belgrove that followed the contemporary fashion for streamlining. It was known as the Gloria Free-Flow and featured a V-shaped split windscreen, the shape of which continued across the roof of the car and swept down along the tail. It was, perhaps, a step too far for the car-buying public in 1935 and although a very small number of examples were completed, the model was removed from the 1936 catalogue and quietly forgotten. It was, however, an early example of the stylish Grand Touring car – one that has power and comfort with the ability to traverse long distances.

The First Dolomite

Meanwhile, Healey, influenced perhaps by Alfa-Romeo, specified the design of a new model to be named Dolomite that was to be powered by a 2-litre eight-cylinder supercharged inline engine. Introduced in late 1934, Healey competed in the 1935 Monte-Carlo Rally with one of these cars but retired early from the event following a *contretemps* with a railway train while driving through Denmark.

With no experience of building such engines, Healey was able to purchase an Alfa-Romeo and make a study of the engine, enabling the Triumph engine to be designed and constructed. Healey always emphasised that the design was 'close to' that of the Italian marque and neither a clone nor reverse-engineered example, saying that Alfa-Romeo were 'extremely helpful'. Featuring huge brake drums, the design was clearly intended for performance and is quoted as developing 120bhp, with transmission being by way of a Wilson pre-selector gearbox. Only three cars were ever completed: the first was the car prepared for the Monte-Carlo rally, fitted with cycle wings to the front wheels; the second, another complete car; and the third featured a chrome-plated chassis for exhibition.

There were drawings for various large coach-built bodies, but none of these were made or the designs actually finalised. A 2-litre motor car that could attain and maintain speeds of 100mph in 1935 had the potential to be the finest car that Triumph ever produced, being as fast, if not faster, than contemporary Lagondas and Bentleys. Nothing was known

One of the three original Dolomite models is seen here competing at one of the many classic competition events.

Above: The front view of the first Dolomite. The large brake drums are visible, and the radiator grille follows the Triumph style with the globe emblem and the word 'Dolomite' underneath.

Below: The driver's view shows the easily readable instruments and typically large steering wheel. The lever to the right of the steering column is the control for the Wilson pre-select gearbox, while what appears to be the clutch pedal is used to activate the previously selected gear.

of the existence of these cars between 1939 and 1979, when the two completed cars were discovered, and both have been restored.

From 1936, the Dolomite name was again used on a wider range of saloon and open cars, now powered with Triumph's own four- or six-cylinder overhead valve engines. Differing from the previous Coventry-Climax-sourced power plants, the Triumph design used overhead valves for both inlet and exhaust, unlike the Climax engines of the time that continued to use an inlet over exhaust arrangement. Triumph stated that the new arrangement, especially with inlet and exhaust manifolds on opposite sides of the engine in a crossflow arrangement, provided for better engine cooling and easier maintenance. The gearbox now featured synchromesh on all forward gears, except bottom gear, but with Triumph not having its own gear-cutting capability, the gear wheels were bought in from Austin.

A distinctive feature of Walter Belgrove's Dolomite design was the radiator grille, known as a 'waterfall grille' and designed in the fashionable art deco style. It was the first time that a die-cast radiator grille had been used on any British-built car. For the more conservative motorists for whom this styling was, perhaps, far too racy and adventurous, a more traditional-looking model with a simpler grille was also available under the model name Vitesse. The Dolomite styling then had a distinctly transatlantic appearance. Belgrove was also advancing his ideas that a motor car should have an overall style set by the designer, with the chassis, mechanical and body construction being designed to fit that overall style rather than the more traditional approach where each department undertook their own design within a given set of dimensional parameters almost in isolation, with the stylist hoping to amalgamate the outcome into a homogeneous design.

The Dolomite name was used again on this later range featuring the avant-garde 'waterfall' radiator grille.

While the new Dolomite showed off the very latest in car styling, this saloon model of the same period is more restrained and badged as a 'Vitesse'. Both Dolomite and Vitesse model names would be reused much later in the history of Triumph.

The new Dolomite and Vitesse models marked a period of success for Triumph, with the company actually earning a profit for once following the disposal of the motorcycle business. Looking to the future, thoughts turned to finding a partner company with whom the costs of assembly could be shared. As Healey still had good relations with his former employer, Riley, discussions commenced with a view to a form of partnership of equals either by merger or acquisition. In hindsight, it is difficult to understand how either partner could benefit as the two companies' product ranges were competitive and, other than those of scaling, it is difficult to see what advantages might have accrued. However, the discussions proved academic as Riley was placed into receivership in February 1938 and purchased outright by Lord Nuffield, later to be sold into the Nuffield Group.

Of all the Dolomite and Vitesse models, the most significant sports car product and visually distinctive was the Dolomite Roadster Coupé, a type again used by Donald Healey for his sporting endeavours. This model, filling a place as both a sports car and grand tourer, included a number of features that were unusual in such a car of that era: behind the front seats an area could be opened to provide two additional seats, wind-up windows were provided and a wide range of colour finishes were listed. The six-cylinder version produced a claimed 75bhp, providing a top speed in the region of 80mph. In 1939, the car cost £450, but this must be set against the average income of the time being in the region of £175.

While many commentators considered Triumph's car of the late 1930s to be among of the finest available at the time, the inability to finance larger production facilities meant that cars were almost being built to order and the economies of scale could not be obtained. It should be noted nevertheless that Triumph were amongst a small group of motor

Above: The large area behind the front seats – shown here with the hood raised, perhaps in anticipation of wet weather – could be opened to provide additional seating capacity.

Left: A rear view of the Dolomite clearly shows the space that could be opened for additional passengers. (De Facto, CC BY-SA)

companies who had survived from the early pioneering days, with most others having fallen by the wayside either as a result of insolvency or acquisition. With war looming, Triumph's spare capacity that arose as a result of selling the motorcycle business was turned over to the production of aircraft engine components. With the finances not showing any improvement and being unable to obtain the necessary finance to fund the volume production necessary, it was only a short time before the inevitable occurred: the company's bankers finally lost patience and receivers were shortly appointed. A saviour in the form of Thomas Ward & Co., a general engineering business based in Sheffield, was found in the short term, and during the war years the company was focussed entirely on the production of armaments to support the war effort. With the production facilities and tooling destroyed by enemy action, the company was again put up for sale. It was acquired by the Standard Motor Company late in 1944, and Triumph ceased to be an independent company.

2

Triumph Roadster and TRX

Now a part of what would eventually be called Standard-Triumph, little if anything beyond the Triumph company name and goodwill survived. However, Sir John Black had a desire to produce a range of sports cars to complement the company's established range of saloons. Building on the expertise developed with aero engineering during the war years, these cars would be 'cars of Style and Distinction', to quote from an announcement made by Standard. Crucially, it would allow the Standard company to compete with William Lyons' company, previously known as SS Cars but now known simply as Jaguar. For many years Standard had supplied Lyons' company with sub-assemblies, including complete engines. Sir John had a long-held ambition to compete in the same market. The acquisition of the Triumph name and prestige provided an opportunity for this wish to come to fruition.

Early post-war production for all manufacturers was a continuation of a reduced range of models that had been in production in 1939, sometimes with minor changes, but all the time with production severely limited by the scarcity of materials. Standard's immediate post-war range was comprised of lightly revised late 1930s Flying Standard models, but it was decided that with the necessary equipment having been destroyed, a totally new Triumph model would be needed. The United Kingdom's government strongly prioritised export markets, especially those that would earn money to aid in the repayment of the war debt. Standard would address this need with its 'world car' then in design and which would reach the market in 1948 as the Vanguard. Triumph would produce a new model in the sports car or roadster mould, alongside a saloon model that later in its production life shared some common assemblies of the Vanguard, but with an entirely different body style that owed nothing to any previous cars to carry the Triumph badge.

Triumph Roadster

Focussing now on the gestation of the Triumph Roadster, a car that fitted the definition of a sports car of the period, the mechanicals were entirely Standard items. The four-cylinder, overhead-valve engine of 1,776cc was of the type built by Standard and also supplied to Jaguar, with the gearbox utilised from the existing reintroduced Flying Standard range.

The gear linkage was adapted to allow for a column gear change. The Flying Standard also provided the rear axle and front suspension, but the chassis was of a new design. Ideally, the chassis design would likely have been traditionally constructed with sheet steel pressings, but government restrictions on the availability of sheet steel, which was urgently needed for replacement of housing lost during the conflict, would make this impossible, so a different solution was mandated. Tubular steel was available in quantity and as Standard had perfected methods of assembling tubular steel sections (gathered during experience building aircraft) and had a workforce skilled in this practice, it was the obvious solution. Tooling and jigging was quite basic, with the car not being considered as either a volume or long-term model. All that was now required was a body.

At this time, Walter Belgrove remained engaged with aircraft work for the government and so the task to style the body fell to Frank Callaby, with Sir John providing an outline of what he wanted to be produced. During the late 1930s, Sir John had owned one of William Lyons' SS100 cars and made it quite clear that he wanted his new roadster to be equally low, sleek and exciting. Following the usual process of early sketches to be shown to management for approval, a design was agreed and work could commence on engineering designs. A specific feature that Sir John was extremely keen on, and adamant that it would be included, was the 'dickey' or 'rumble' seat, reminiscent of the last pre-war Triumph Roadster models. Indeed, the new Triumph Roadster was to be the final car to be designed

Triumph's Roadster of the immediate post-war period owed much of its styling to the pre-war period.

Above: A low, front view of the Roadster emphasises the large headlamps, spot lamps and horns along with the long bonnet, which were all characteristic of the model.

Below: Clearly demonstrating the dickey seat in operation. Note the reinforced steps on the rear bumper to aid passengers in accessing the rear of the car, also the windscreen protection that folded out.

with such an anachronistic feature. The finalised design included doors hinged from the B post, a style that has since become known as 'suicide doors'. The seat was a full three-seater, and it had a low, wide windscreen – three wipers were required. The design, considered unattractive by many, was an example of a car designed by two people. Callaby provided all the detail drawings from the B post forward, while his colleague and senior draftsman Arthur Ballard worked on the B post rewards, including the dickey seat and hood shape and mechanism. However, Callaby had responsibility for the overall styling.

Left: The width of the front seat can be seen here, providing room for three-abreast seating. Note the column gear change, unusually set to the right of the steering wheel.

Below: A rear view showing the erected hood. The unusual windscreen for the dicky seat can be seen in the closed position.

With the shortage of sheet steel, Triumph's pre-war techniques for the body assembly were adopted, with the aluminium body skins pressed in-house by Standard-Triumph and mounted on an ash frame. This individualistic approach to assembly was hugely at odds with Standard's existing range and that of its pre-war years, whereby bodies had been built by outside suppliers constructed from steel pressings and supplied assembled ready for mounting onto the chassis, but with the shortages described there was no alternative. Customers could choose from three colours for the car: Black with beige upholstery, Dark Metallic Grey with blue upholstery or Maroon with red upholstery. The folding hood could be supplied in Black or Fawn for the Black or Maroon finish, and Black or Grey for the Metallic Grey car. Matching cushions were also supplied for the dickey seat, which also featured a fold-out windscreen section fitted with safety glass, giving an unusual part-glazed finish to the luggage compartment when the extra seat was not in use.

This, then, was the car that was designated 18TR and would remain in production from 1946 until 1948. The 1948 model, designated 20TR, would benefit from various mechanical changes, the most significant being a new engine and gearbox. As is widely known, Standard-Triumph had engaged in an agreement with the Ferguson company to build agricultural tractors. As part of this agreement a new engine had been designed – the well-known and respected Standard 'wet-liner' engine. Despite the tractor and car engines having substantial differences, they did share some components that would make the engine a staple part of the Standard-Triumph range far into the future. Initially launched in the Vanguard (the Standard 'world car'), it made sense to also use this engine

With the rear compartment open, two small folding seats can be seen, ahead of which is space for the passenger's feet. When additional passengers were carried, luggage capacity was limited.

in the Roadster. Utilising wet liners, it was a relatively simple task to specify differing swept capacities depending on application, but for the Roadster the same capacity as the Vanguard – 2,088cc – was specified. Along with the engine, a new gearbox, now with three speeds, was adopted. It still used a column change, but this was now mounted left of the steering column. Repositioning the gear-change lever made the car more conventional, but did mean that the driver needed care with gear changes when a central passenger was carried. While the 18TR had a quoted power of 64bhp, the 20TR increased this slightly to 68bhp. In total, the build records show that 4,501 Roadsters of both 18TR and 20TR designations were completed before production ended in September 1949. The car that was intended to follow was as avant garde as the Roadster had been, a revival of a previous era.

TR-X

The replacement for the Roadster was given the working code name of TR-X. Walter Belgrove, now released from his earlier war work, took responsibility for the overall design of this new car. The ambition had been to design a vehicle that could compete on equal terms with Jaguar's newly announced XK120 model which was launched as an open car at the 1948 London Motor Show. The concept for the new model, especially the desire for it to compete head-to-head with Jaguar, came directly from Sir John Black.

An example of an early Jaguar XK fixed-head coupé model. The desire of Sir John Black to compete with Jaguar in this market was ultimately to lead to the Triumph TR.

Belgrove was given a free hand in the design of the new model – those familiar with the constraints imposed on Belgrove in his designs for the Standard Vanguard will understand as meaning he did what Sir John wanted. The first prerequisite was that the new car would be based on the chassis of the Vanguard, dictating a wheelbase of 94 inches. Sensibly, Vanguard running gear was utilised, although the 2,088cc wet-liner engine was fitted with twin carburettors providing a maximum output of 71bhp, an increase of just 3bhp over the bigger and heavier saloon. However, overdrive was now available, something that had never been available on the earlier Roadster. A multitude of new features were intended to be fitted, including a built-in hydraulic jacking system, electro-hydraulic adjustable seats, windows and mechanism to raise and lower the hood, a powered aerial and headlights hidden behind a metal shield that was, again, electrically operated.

The full-fronted body styling was rounded and included numerous double-curved panels, many of which were double-skinned. With the continued limitations on the availability of steel, it was envisaged that the body would be formed from aluminium. It would have been possible for the prototypes to have been built in-house, but Sir John gave the job to the firm of Helliwells Ltd of Walsall, who were instructed to provide three such completed bodies in time for the completed cars to be exhibited at the 1949 London Motor Show. Despite encouragement both from Walter Belgrove and Sir John, Helliwells were slow in the execution of the order. So much so that it became clear that the 1949 deadline was going to be missed. Consequently, the part-finished bodies were brought back to Standard-Triumph facilities at Banner Lane, where the work was completed. It transpired that Halliwells, who were experienced in the construction of aircraft, were applying the same level of detail, care and precision to what was, in effect, a prototype car that they would normally use on a production aircraft.

Now completed, the new model was shown first at the 1950 Paris Motor Show and later at the London Motor Show held at Earl's Court. As a concession to Belgrove, the cars featured an initial letter 'B' behind the front wheel arch, identifying him as the car's stylist. The public's reaction was mixed, with Triumph's own sales staff remaining to be convinced that the car was destined for showroom success. The motoring press, as was normal at that time, praised the car, with enough interest generated by visitors for the company to seriously consider putting it into production. One obstacle, though, would be price: with a base price of £975, it would be the most expensive Triumph or Standard ever, equivalent to more than double the average annual income and in line with the Jaguar. A slightly embarrassing incident occurred at the London Show when the stand was visited by Princess Margaret, who asked to see some of the advanced features demonstrated, at which point they failed with an ominous emission of smoke, indicating burning electrics.

With hindsight, it is easy to question why so much overly sophisticated technology was put into a car at a time of such shortage and austerity. Perhaps the intention was to support the 'export or die' mantra of the government of the time, and to use the model as a money earner in the United States market. Across the West Midlands, in Longbridge, Austin had also engaged in a similar exercise with their Austin A90 Atlantic model. The Atlantic was a failure, with just 350 cars selling in the US and, with rapidly changing tastes, it was equally likely that the Triumph TR-X could have met the same fate.

Above: An extremely rare surviving TR-X. (Ron Cromer, Triumph Roadster Club)

Left: Austin produced the A90 Atlantic at the same time as Triumph's TR-X, and there are similarities in overall design. The USA was the intended market, but it was not a success. Examples today are rare.

A further obstacle to the car going into production was the lack of resources for it to be produced, with Standard-Triumph's own resources being committed to the design of the Phase 2 Vanguard and a new, small car. With this in mind, Belgrove was dispatched on two missions to Italy, first to meet with Carrozzeria Touring and later with Pininfarina, with a view to either one producing bodyshells. No agreement was reached, however, and it was realised that TR-X was not destined for production. It was not such a sad ending, though, as the team who had been employed on TR-X rapidly found themselves engaged on a new project code-named '20TS'.

3

The Sidescreen TRs

Sir John Black remained ambitious to create a new sports car that took full advantage of the Triumph brand. Early discussions with William Lyons at Jaguar, who remained an important customer for Standard engines, regarding a joint enterprise were unsuccessful. An approach to Morgan, possibly even a complete takeover, were equally unsuccessful. So, the only viable alternative was for Standard-Triumph to create their own model.

The specification dictated a two-seater car to be launched at the 1952 London Show with a 2-litre engine, a target price of £500 and a maximum speed of 90mph. Walter Belgrove was tasked with the overall styling and Harry Webster was responsible for the mechanical layout. Webster had joined 'the Standard' at the age of fifteen and by 1948 had risen to become chief chassis engineer. He would go on to become a significant contributor to the entire Triumph product family.

With both time and financial pressures, it made good sense to review the existing cars being produced to see what could be re-utilised and adapted for the new project. The front suspension came from the Triumph Mayflower, a small, two-door saloon that shared a similar design to the larger Triumph Renown model. The Mayflower also provided the basis for the rear axle, although this needed to be reduced in width to suit the new sports car. The wet-liner engine, now fitted with liners to provide a capacity of 1,991cc, was to provide power and the gearbox, originally designed for the Vanguard but now with four forward speeds and a floor change, was specified. This then left the question of a chassis. A stock of spare pre-war Standard Flying Nine chassis was discovered, which provided the basis for the new chassis. It was decided to mount the axle above the side rails of the chassis, a decision that was to have serious consequences within a short period of time.

Body styling occurred in parallel to the mechanical specification. It was a low car with cutaway doors and, setting a style for TRs for many years, inset headlamps positioned on the front apron rather than directly in front of the wheels. The rear was rounded with an externally mounted spare wheel that featured the fuel filler protruding from its centre to fill a rear-mounted fuel tank. This meant that there was no luggage capacity. The price target was missed by around 10 per cent, with the base price now being £555 and, with purchase tax, an on-the-road price of £865. Officially titled 20TS, the car was launched to an eager public on the same day that Donald Healey, having left Triumph and now running his own business, announced a new model. Very shortly after he would enter an agreement with the Austin Company for them to manufacture the car that became the Austin-Healey.

Following the London Motor Show launch of the new car, where reactions to the styling had been mixed with comments particularly concerning the lack of luggage space, a group of motoring journalists were invited to test the new car, but initial reports were anything but encouraging. Particular concerns mentioned road holding, the extremely firm ride and flexing of the chassis.

Back to the Drawing Board

To obtain an external, expert opinion, well-known race car and engine designer Ken Richardson was asked to appraise the car. His opinion was extremely negative, with various reports noting he described it as 'a death trap' and 'the most awful car I have ever driven'. It was time for a rethink.

Richardson was then invited to join the design team for the car, and his experience in development would be extremely beneficial. First came changes to the chassis, with enhanced stiffening of the cruciform, followed by larger brakes. Reworking the engine breathing by way of modified valve timings and increasing the compression ratio improved the power from 75bhp to 90bhp – a significant statistic as it was now identical to the Austin-Healey 100, except where the Healey required 2,660cc to develop that power, the Triumph could achieve it with just 1,991cc, allowing it to compete in the under-2-litre class in sport events.

The comments regarding the bodywork, especially to the rear of the car, were taken seriously, resulting in Belgrove developing a new style that repositioned the fuel tank over the rear axle and provided a proper luggage compartment, with the spare wheel now located in its own lockable compartment below the boot. Launched to the public at the Geneva Motor Show in March 1953, this was the new Triumph sports car, now officially named TR2, which would become a familiar sight on the roads and, with just detail modification, would continue in production for ten years.

It was a busy period for sports car launches: the Austin-Healey arrived at the same time, as did the Rootes Group's new Sunbeam Alpine. The Rootes Group, always looking for a marketing opportunity, took their new model to Belgium, where the newly built Jabekke motorway was utilised for a demonstration run that captured the interest of enthusiasts. Having a larger engine, but developing 10bhp less than the Triumph's 90bhp, Sir John Black rose to the challenge of beating the achievement and made arrangements for Ken Richardson to take an early prototype car to Belgium with the aim of beating the Alpine and in the process set a speed record. The car was lightly modified by removing the windscreen and fitting a single aero screen, removing the driver's seat and providing little more than a floor cushion for Richardson to sit on, fitting rear wheel spats and a metal tonneau cover and removing the bumpers. In this trim, a speed of just over 104mph was achieved, but then it was discovered that the engine was only running on three cylinders. Rectified, a further test run achieved a speed of 124.889mph, just exceeding 200kph and setting a world record for a 2-litre car. In a publicity film released by Standard-Triumph, the well-known former RAF pilot, rally driver, journalist and later TV personality Raymond

Above: TS2, as this car is known, commemorating its commission number, was the first right-hand-drive TR2 to be produced.

Below: TS2 was originally sold in the Republic of Ireland, shown here. It is wearing its original Irish registration. The poor visibility with the original hood in place is clear to see.

Seen at a large classic car show is the actual car that was used for the record-setting Jabekke highway run.

Baxter told the world that the car had achieved 'what had been planned – the fastest under two litre sports car of its price'.

Production got off to a slow but steady start, with around 250 cars being produced in 1953. While final assembly of the completed cars was undertaken by Standard-Triumph, most of the assemblies were sub-contracted. Chassis were originally pressed from sheet steel, now available in adequate quantities, by Sankey and shipped to Canley for assembly until such point as Sankey were supplied with the necessary jigs to assemble complete chassis. The bodywork was pressed and assembled by Mulliners, a business with a long tradition of working with Standard. Electrical components came from Lucas.

Unlike comments published on the earlier Roadsters, TR-X and 20TS, the press were very complimentary about the car. Motor sport achievements came swiftly, with an outright win by John Wallwork driving a TR2 in the 1954 RAC Rally. In total, fourteen TR2s entered the event and only one failed to finish, providing a compelling reassurance for the performance and ruggedness of the new car. Triumph also brought home a good haul of silverware following the 1954 Rallye des Alpes, with TR2s winning second, third and fourth places in the 2-litre class.

A few detail design changes were to follow. The bonnet material was changed from aluminium to steel, and the original rasping exhaust note was tamed by use of a longer

Above and below: Both cars seen here were originally 'works' competition cars for Triumph. Both still compete in period events.

A very early production TR2 that is much used by its long-time owner. The 'long' doors can be seen.

silencer. The biggest change, however, was a redesign of the doors and, consequently, the sills. The doors originally extended to the lowest extremes of the car, which could present a problem if it were to be parked against a high kerb as it would either be impossible to open the door or the door skin could come into contact with the ground, causing damage. To overcome this, conventional sills were fitted and the door length was reduced. For 1955, the rear brake drum size was increased to give more powerful braking, and the overdrive control was now operated by a toggle switch and worked on all but reverse and first gear, electrically interlocked to prevent inadvertent selection. A hard top became available, and the removable soft top was fitted with rear-quarter windows, providing much improved rear three-quarter vision when driving with the soft roof in place. A new bonnet lock was fitted using budget locks operated by a tee key, which was also needed to open the boot and spare wheel compartment. Door locks were not fitted, neither were external handles, in line with normal practice for open cars; it would be some years before such basic security features were considered necessary. Standard-Triumph could reflect that their new little sports car was a good dollar earner, with more than 70 per cent of production being exported.

The year 1955 also brought success for Triumph at Le Mans, despite the tragedies that had occurred in the event. Three cars had been entered and all three finished, but what is of greater significance is that the TRs were essentially the same cars that the customer would be able to purchase shortly after the event.

Wearing its weather equipment, this is a later TR2 clearly showing the modification to produce a 'short' door. By this time, the rain hood had gained rear quarter-transparent panels.

TR2 Becomes TR3

For the 1955 London Motor Show, the TR was modified sufficiently that a name revision was thought advantageous, with the TR2 evolving into TR3. Cosmetically, the most striking change was at the front of the car, where a metal grille now covered the open-mouth appearance of the TR2, along with a change in the wing beading from body colour paint finish to stainless steel and hinges now being chrome finish. The weather-protecting side screens now had a sliding section, and a rear seat was added to the options list. There were significant changes under the bonnet: power was raised to 95bhp by utilising larger carburettors, though almost immediately afterwards this would increase to 100bhp, with a new cylinder head. This latter modification followed Triumph's success in the Le Mans endurance race earlier in the year. Also fitted for the Le Mans event were disc brakes, cutting-edge technology at the time and normally only seen on much more exotic machinery. For the 1957 model year, front disc brakes became a standard fit on the TR3, making it the first production sports car to be so fitted and giving a clear lead over the rival Austin-Healey that would be two years behind in adopting the technology.

A further set of revisions followed in January 1958 with the final set of styling changes made to the TR3, which became known as TR3A, although Standard-Triumph were officially

Above: A TR3 can be most easily recognised by the new grille. The side screens now have sliding windows.

Below: Under the bonnet of the TR3. This car had been specially prepared at the factory for the London Motor Show and has been retained exactly as built.

Above: The rear seat was an option. It was useful for carrying children, but very cramped for adults.

Below: The cockpit shows the simple but effective layout of instruments and toggle overdrive switch at the right-hand extremity of the dashboard.

much slower in adopting the new name. The most visually obvious change occurred at the front of the car, where a new full-width chrome grille was added. A secondary, more subtle change was made to the headlights, which were now slightly recessed into the front apron. The Triumph name was now fitted to the front apron, just below the model badge, so there could be no doubt about the pedigree of the car. Making life easier for owners, the doors were at last fitted with locking handles, as was the luggage compartment, but the bonnet and spare wheel cover kept their budget locks, so it was wise for the owner to still carry the key.

Above: Being cornered with some enthusiasm, this TR3A shows the optional hard top that was available for the side-screen TRs.

Left: Showing the wide, 'grinning' grille fitted to the TR3A with the maker's name emblazoned just above.

With the TR3A, the car finally gained external door handles with locks.

Anticipating strong sales, production of the latest cars was commenced three months or so prior to announcement, ensuring a ready stock of cars to fulfil the anticipated customer orders, especially for export. Triumph's expectations were met with 16,000 cars rolling off the line in 1958. The competition from MG and especially Austin-Healey had also moved on, with the Healey now powered by a 2.6-litre six-cylinder engine which was increased to 2.9 litres during 1958. MG had moved on from their very traditional T models and could now offer the MGA, but while the Triumph and big Healey gained success in motor sport, the MGA did not. To maximise the success in sports events, the TR had been designed to be eligible as an under-2-litre car, but changes, especially in rallying, were occurring that permitted an increase in engine capacity and, accordingly, an engine with a capacity of 2,138cc was introduced as an option.

With the side-screen TRs now in production for seven years, thoughts were turning to a replacement model, but the company's finances were taking a turn for the worse. The tractor manufacturing agreement for Ferguson had come to an end, with Standard-Triumph using the cash from it to purchase strategically important component suppliers. This was an era when all manufacturers were securing their production through tighter control of suppliers, and it was unfortunate for Standard-Triumph that this period coincided with a downturn in world markets, especially domestically. Production of all Standard products, as well as the TR, was rapidly reduced to allow unsold models to be sold. It was beginning to look like the 1930s again, and it was quite likely that the TR3A would be the end of sports cars from Standard-Triumph.

In what appears to be something of a recurring theme for the company, a saviour was found in Leyland Motors Ltd, well-known and highly regarded manufacturer of large commercial vehicles who were looking to enter the car business. They should not be confused with British Leyland, which shall enter the story much later.

The plans for a new sports car were approved, but one last revision of the TR3 was to come first for US markets. With America providing such a lucrative market for TRs, it made sense to gather dealer opinion on what would, and could, be sold. Their feedback on the new proposal was not positive, so a compromise was reached. Triumph would introduce the new model but the sidescreen car would continue to be sold, though only in the United States. This car was officially known as TR3B. All TR3B cars were fitted with a revised gearbox intended for the newer model, now with synchromesh on all four forward gears. The first 500 cars built were fitted with 1,991cc engines, and the balance with 2,138cc engines.

A second option was considered to satisfy the concerns of the dealer network for a continuation of the sidescreen cars. What looked at first glance to be another TR3A was constructed on the new chassis that would underpin the next TR. As the new chassis design was wider than the existing TR3A, it was necessary to revise the frontal view of the car, but the changes were minor visually. After two prototype cars code-named Beta had been constructed, the project was not continued.

Although not an original car, this replica Beta shows the changes applied to the wider chassis design, with the combined front marker and turn lamps now fitted to the wings rather than being inset to the grille.

4

Triumph Spitfire

The design for a small, low-price sports car had been in place for some years prior to it entering production. To understand its origin, it is necessary to jump backwards a few years and examine its beginnings. During the earlier part of the 1950s, a new small car was launched as the Standard 8. This was intended to compete with BMC's Austin A30 and Morris Minor, but early versions of the car carried 'economy' to a degree previously unseen, with anything that was not a legal obligation removed. Later cars were more generously equipped and a larger 10hp model soon joined the range. A replacement model was scheduled for 1959, which would be an entirely different car, but would continue to use the engine and gearbox from the final iteration of the 8hp and 10hp family. Alongside the design of this new small car, the Standard Vanguard Phase 3 was being facelifted. The work on this was outsourced to Vignale in Italy as a result of the young and highly talented stylist Giovanni Michelotti being introduced to Standard-Triumph. The design for the new small car, which was realised with a remarkably quick turnaround time, was launched in 1959 as the Triumph Herald. Standard-Triumph encountered difficulties: many of the usual bodywork suppliers either fell into the ownership of rival car companies or they were unable to quote for the job due to full order books. This resulted in the Herald being built on a traditional chassis and the coachwork constructed from large subassemblies that could easily be interchanged, allowing the Herald to be built as a two-door saloon, coupé, convertible and estate car.

It was from an adaptation of these basic building blocks that the new sports car was to be derived. It was again styled by Michelotti, but with the financial turmoil prior to the Leyland Motors takeover the prototype was discovered in the works and rushed into production for a 1962 launch. The design brief called for a two-door open sports car that would compete with the Austin-Healey Sprite, a small two-seater car that used the mechanical underpinnings from the Austin A30. Later versions of the Sprite would share many features with a very similar model being produced by MG under the Midget brand, giving rise to the description of the two models as 'Spridget'.

Origins of the Spitfire

The new sports car's chassis was based on a shortened Herald chassis with a narrow, central backbone. To provide additional strength, the Spitfire featured structural door sills, making the production car very true to Michelotti's original design. The only obvious changes were the raised height of the door tops, to accommodate completely retractable windows, and the instruments and switches being positioned in the centre of the dashboard to standardise the layout for both left- and right-hand-drive builds.

Mechanically, the front suspension came directly from the Herald and therefore continued the use of coil springs and dual wishbones, originally used in the Standard 8 (1953), with the rear suspension retaining the transverse leaf spring, swinging-arm arrangement of the Herald. With the Spitfire lacking the chassis cross members of the Herald, the pivot for the suspension now needed to be bodyshell mounted. Driven fiercely, this arrangement could cause a degree of oversteer, which could become terminal if power was removed while cornering. This was not something specific to the Spitfire, however, as most other cars that utilised a similar suspension set-up revealed the same handling characteristics.

Power came from the Herald's 1,147cc engine, now fitted with twin carburettors, developing 63bhp and making the car capable of achieving 90mph, delivered through a four-speed gearbox with overdrive soon added as an option. Factory options added not long into the production run included a steel hard top and wire wheels. A cabin heater was also listed as an optional extra, perhaps not seen as essential in a car that would likely be used for the majority of the time as an open car. One valuable feature, shared with the Herald,

An advantage of the centrally mounted instruments was that production for left- and right-hand drive was simplified. The interior of the Spitfire was more refined and comfortable than that of alternatives on the market at the time for a comparable price. (Akele NDE, CC BY-SA)

was a one-piece, forward-hinged bonnet that when opened allowed simple access to the engine and front suspension, to the extent that a front wheel provided a comfortable place to sit when servicing the engine. The external seams to the bonnet were finished with a bright embellisher.

The bodywork was constructed locally in Coventry by the firm Forward Radiator, and the styling was so successful that it remained with only minor changes throughout the production life of the Spitfire. The soft top was of the type that could be removed from the car entirely, rather than a folding 'pram type'. Badges were kept simple, with the rear of the car displaying the script 'Spitfire 4', giving many commentators thoughts as to whether a six-cylinder-powered Spitfire might be in future plans.

Right: Although the engine has been modified from standard, this image shows the ease of access to both the engine and front suspension of the Spitfire's design. (Colin Radford)

Below: An example of a US model of an early Spitfire 4, photographed in the delightful setting of Palm Springs, California. (Rex Gray, CC BY-SA)

Rear view of a different Spitfire 4, demonstrating the simplicity of design. The reversing lights are an aftermarket addition. The use of the Spitfire 4 badging would cause confusion in future years once the Mk IV Spitfire was launched. (Akele NDE, CC BY-SA)

Spitfire Evolution

An Mk II Spitfire arrived in early 1965 with little change, just a new diaphragm spring clutch, a small increase in engine power to 67bhp and detail changes to the cabin and, of course, a change in badges to denote that the car was now a Spitfire Mk II.

Two years later, the model was revised again to create the Spitfire Mk III. Looking from the front of the car, the most obvious change was the raising of the front bumper height in compliance with new United States regulations so that it now sat in front of the radiator grille. Under the bonnet was a new, larger cylinder bore engine of 1,296cc capacity, still with twin carburettors but now with a reworked cylinder head to provide more efficient gas flow and, consequently, more power, with an output of 75bhp being quoted. This was enough to propel the car to 100mph – a very exhilarating experience in such a small, open car and one that ensured it would continue to sell in good numbers, with Triumph celebrating the 100,000th Spitfire being built at the end of 1967. As an improvement to driver and passenger comfort, especially in countries that experience inclement weather, a new folding hood was now fitted that could be raised or lowered in less time than the previous arrangement of roof sticks and covers.

Above: Externally, the Mk II Spitfire differed very little to its predecessor.

Below: While at the rear, the only change apparent is the substitution of the Mk II badge.

The Spitfire Mk III is immediately recognisable by the raised height of the front bumper. The folded roof now remains attached to the car and can be seen at the rear of the cockpit under its cover. (Colin Radford)

Production had now reached a point where the press tools were beginning to wear, and with essentially the same car having been on sale for over five years, thoughts were given to a restyle, a task once again given to Michelotti, whose brief required the centre section of the existing model to be retained with changes limited to the front and rear sections. His new design resulted in visually little change to the front of the car. Pop-up headlights had been considered but were discarded when changes to American regulations suggested that such features might be outlawed. One very apparent change resulted in the bonnet gaining a much cleaner design, with the earlier seams now removed and the contours of the wings being smoothed into the bonnet. Inside the car, the central instrument panel was located to be positioned in front of the driver. At the rear, the Spitfire now featured a flat boot lid, with the fuel filler remaining located centrally on the rear deck. A new cut-off rear that followed the style of other designs being worked for Triumph was also employed, giving a very crisp, modern and highly distinctive design. Also included in the new design was a revised hard top, now squarer with rear quarter windows and a flatter roof. The new model, still badged as a Spitfire, now sported badges announcing it as Mk IV, the choice of Roman numerals reducing any confusion with the original car that, now rather confusingly, had been badged with a '4' as part of its model name.

Above and below: The advent of the Spitfire Mk IV brought a smoother and more modern finish to the front wings.

It was underneath the car at the rear that the most important mechanical change had been made. With growing criticism of the car's handling when cornering with enthusiasm, Triumph revised the rear suspension so that the transverse leaf spring was now able to pivot on top of the differential casing, reducing suspension geometry changes to a minimum. Finally, a revised gearbox with synchromesh on all forward gears was now fitted with overdrive still available as a very sensible option. One unfortunate side effect of tightening legislation regarding exhaust emissions in the United States, still a very important market for Triumph, resulted in the Spitfire being increasingly restricted in terms of power output, with power outputs as low 48bhp being quoted for US-bound cars towards the end of the Spitfire Mk IV's life.

Spitfire 1500

The final iteration for the Spitfire came at the end of 1974 when the familiar mark numbering system also ended, with the replacement car now badged as Spitfire 1500, reflecting the fact that it was now powered by an engine of 1493cc, derived from the earlier engines that could trace their heritage back to the Standard 8 of the middle 1950s. The increased capacity was achieved by lengthening the stroke which also increased its torque, thus making the car easier to drive in city centre traffic. To slightly confuse the issue, this same engine had powered the earlier Mk IV car for North American markets from the previous year as a way to overcome the emissions control-related power reductions that affected the 1,296cc engine. Badges for the revised car were now vinyl with a large 'Spitfire 1500' placed on the bonnet. Most of the changes were minor, with one noticeable change being the addition of cloth sections to the seats in a bright houndstooth check pattern. The switch gear was tidied with a move from dashboard-mounted switches to column-mounted

Now in its final iteration, the Spitfire 1500 shown here wears the new vinyl identification and shows the factory hard top.

Above: Viewed sideways on, the Spitfire styling was still clearly recognisable and demonstrated a clear connection between the first Spitfire 4 and final Spitfire 1500, as seen here.

Below: This Spitfire 1500 demonstrates the improved folding roof introduced earlier in the car's life. The boot-mounted rack was a very popular accessory for touring to accommodate more luggage.

stalks and, in keeping with the fashion of the time, the brightwork (such as windscreen wipers and door mirrors) was now presented in a matt black finish. The new finish was claimed by some to have a safety benefit as it was less prone to cause distracting dazzle.

In the United States emission controls became even tighter, resulting in a situation where the car could no longer meet the legislation and, consequently, was quietly withdrawn from that market. The knock-on effect of this on production volumes resulted in a decision to withdraw the Spitfire from the market entirely, with the final Triumph Spitfire rolling off the production line in August 1980 to mark the end of production of one of the most distinctive small sports cars of its era.

Spitfire or Midget?

For sports car enthusiasts there has always been an element of rivalry, mostly friendly and good humoured, between those who favour MG and those whose car of choice will always be a Triumph. With the Spitfire competing directly against the MG Midget for all of its life, and to a smaller extent against the MGB, there is a certain irony, not overlooked by Triumph aficionados, that the final MG Midgets to be produced were powered not by the original long-serving BMC A series engine, but by a Triumph 1,500cc engine – the same as used in the final Spitfires. The fact that by this time both MG and Triumph were part of the sprawling British Leyland empire is quietly overlooked.

Motor Sport

Triumph Spitfires shared a brief period of factory-sponsored motor sport during 1964 and 1965. Initially, the cars entered into rallying were fitted with standard production hard tops and painted in Wedgwood blue, while the cars for the 24-hour endurance event at Le Mans were given a flowing, fastback style which would later be used on the rally cars. The circuit racing cars were painted in British Racing Green with a distinctive coloured panel at the front of the car to aid easy recognition of the individual cars while racing. A notable early class win came in the 1964 4,000-mile Tour de France rally. In the same year at Le Mans, only one of the three cars entered finished after the other two crashed, with an officially recorded speed of 133mph. Success followed at Sebring with Spitfires in second and third places in their class at the 12-hour race in 1965. At Le Mans in 1965, four Spitfires were entered, with two cars finishing thirteenth and fourteenth overall, but, more importantly, first and second in class.

5

Michelotti TRs

The next evolution of the TR range was not without its challenges. Chief Stylist Walter Belgrove had left the company, and his department was fully employed with the end-of-line lift to the small car – Standard 8/10 range – that would emerge from the studios as the more flamboyantly styled Standard Pennant and its own eventual replacement, the Triumph Herald. But it was clear that the market for sports cars had moved on from the original ideas that had provided the side-screen TRs with the market looking for ever more power and greater refinement along with increased comfort. Several designs had been worked on within Standard-Triumph without gaining management approval, but it was the involvement of Michelotti again who provided the design ideas that would emerge as the TR4.

Michelotti had a reputation of being able to deliver in short timescales. He provided his initial design sketches within two weeks of being commissioned, along with a costed proposal for the full design – the cost of which was far below the equivalent for an in-house design. Unsurprisingly, Michelotti was commissioned to complete the job. A TR3 rolling chassis was shipped to him and the resulting finished design was delivered three months later. This was displayed alongside the existing proposals from Triumph's own designers for management approval. The design met with approval but the production costs for the numerous new features did not, resulting in a rework to the original design. This delay allowed for the planned chassis changes to be finalised, resulting with the wheelbase of the TR3 being retained but the track being increased by 4 inches with rack-and-pinion steering, front disc brakes and retaining the suspension set-up from the TR3.

This, then, provided the final details necessary for the body design to be finalised. The now familiar TR trademarks of hooded headlamps and a rear shoulder at the rear of the doors were implemented, along with a long, front-hinged bonnet that included a power bulge to accommodate the carburettors. Passengers could now enjoy wind-up windows and face-level fresh air ventilation, but the hood reverted to the simple cover on roof sticks style. The instrument layout followed the pattern established with the earlier cars, now set in a full-width dashboard which on early cars was finished in white.

There was no hard top available, but instead Michelotti provided the design for a surrey roof based on a rear glazed panel and a removable top panel, with both metal and fabric covers being supplied. Power for the new TR4 came from a 2,138cc version

Above: A TR4 from early in the production run. Other than being fitted with more modern seats, this car remains true to its original build.

Below: TR4s continued with the general cabin layout of the earlier sidescreen cars. Note the original steering wheel, floor-mounted fly-off handbrake and period radio.

Above and below: Instead of the traditional hard top, the TR4 was designed to provide a 'surrey' roof system. The rear screen was mounted to the car's bodywork while the metal roof could be quickly removed to create an open car.

of the long-serving wet-liner engine, with a 1,991cc option available for the owner who wanted to enter the car in motor sports events in the under-2-litre class. The gearbox now boasted synchromesh on all forward gears, with overdrive remaining as an option, electrically interlocked and functioning on all gears, except bottom and reverse.

When first put on sale in the UK, the cost, including purchase tax, would provide enough change from £1,140 for a few gallons of petrol. Reviews of the car were generally positive, but the suspension did come in for some comment as the market was perhaps expecting more of an evolution from the TR3 style. Special comment was made about the rear wheels losing contact with the road in hard cornering, the ride being harsh on any but the smoothest surfaces and some mentions of body shake. Triumph responded to the criticism of the suspension with a substantial redesign for 1965 in the form of the TR4A.

Independent Rear Suspension Arrives

While the TR4 had been on sale, Triumph also launched an important mid-sized saloon in the form of the Triumph 2000 that featured independent rear suspension. This technology formed the basis of the changes that transformed the TR4 into the TR4A. While the front of the car was fundamentally unchanged mechanically, the centre section of the chassis was strengthened with mountings for cast semi-trailing arms to be attached. Coil springs and lever arm dampers completed the rear suspension arrangements. The differential housing was now fitted to the chassis, and the final drive was provided through exposed half shafts that featured a movable spline to provide suspension movement, along with universal joints inboard and outboard of the shaft.

Again, the North American dealers were concerned about the inevitable price increase that would ensue, so for this market only a TR4A was listed with a beam axle and retaining the leaf springs. Because the chassis design had now changed, the mountings required additional bracketry as production of the earlier TR4 chassis had ended and it was not practical to build two chassis for fundamentally the same car. It proved to be unnecessary as the new suspension system met with the buying public's approval in the US, and the TR4A, now with IRS badging to reflect its advanced suspension, sold well.

Trim and external changes were minor: a new exhaust manifold increased power marginally to 104bhp and twin exhaust pipes gave an easily recognisable change to the rear; the front side lights and indicators were now positioned in a bright fixture to the side of the front wings; the dashboard was now a wooden item; and a return to a pram-style hood now supplemented the optional surrey top. The critics of the original suspension arrangements were more than satisfied, with one magazine writer describing it as a 'miracle'.

Although selling well, it could not be denied that the engine was now nearing twenty years old in technology and had reached the end of its potential to provide more power. The next change to Michelotti's design would see a substantial increase in power being delivered.

Above: A front three-quarter view of the TR4A shows the most obvious difference being the addition of chrome wing embellishment and revised front marker lights and turn signals.

Below: While at the rear, the TR4A proudly boasts that it has independent rear suspension.

Under the bonnet, the same Standard wet-liner engine, now increased in capacity and in a higher state of tune, continued to provide power. This example has the optional remote brake vacuum servo fitted.

The chrome wing embellishment terminated in this bright lamp holder providing a quick and simple differentiation from the earlier TR4.

The TR4A retained the established dashboard arrangement but now finished in wood. The handbrake has been repositioned to the transmission tunnel.

TR4 in Competition

With minimal funding, Triumph set up a new works team that had its first taste of success with the Spitfire at Le Mans and in Alpine rallying. This team – again, with limited access to resources – continued with the TR4. Vehicles were modified as much as possible to increase competitiveness while still remaining within the limits of competition regulations. Changes such as revised exhaust manifolds, fuel delivery by way of dual twin-chock Weber carburettors and a camshaft with a significantly more aggressive profile than a road car were adopted for the fleet of four competition TR4s, all painted Powder Blue and registered with consecutive numbers – 3, 4, 5 and 6 VC. The bodywork was lightened by replacing steel panels with aluminium, and glass was replaced with polycarbonate sheet. The first event entered was the Tulip Rally in 1962, where the three cars entered finished in second, third and fourth in class. The same year, the TR4s achieved a very credible first, second and third in class in the Alpine Rally.

On the racing circuit in the United States, TR4s had memorable success at Sebring in Florida during 1963 when Triumph achieved first, second and fourth in class at the 12-hour endurance race.

4VC was one of the highly successful works TR4s and draws much attention wherever it is displayed.

6

GT6

The Triumph GT6 evolved from another project undertaken by Giovanni Michelotti for Triumph at the beginning of 1963. The brief was for a fastback version of the Spitfire design that was known internally as Spitfire GT4. Later in the year, the completed design was returned to Triumph for consideration. The overall style met with approval, but the additional weight of the extra bodywork meant that the existing Spitfire 1,147cc engine's performance failed to meet expectations, so the project was sidelined. The aerodynamic benefits of the fastback design found its place in 1964 when, now produced in glass fibre, dramatically reducing its weight, it was fitted to the competition Spitfires as described in a previous chapter.

With the Spitfire selling well in all markets, Triumph management reconsidered the GT proposal, but now with more power. As well as the small car engine from the Herald that powered the existing Spitfire and the wet-liner engine now used only in the TR4, Triumph also had a six-cylinder engine in its range that had originally been designed for a range-topping version of the earlier Vanguard III model. Now being used in 2-litre capacity in Triumph's new 2000 saloon, it was also built in a 1,600cc capacity to provide power for another new model, again based on the Herald that, with some design changes, was being introduced as the Triumph Vitesse. In 2-litre format, this engine would provide ample performance for the new GT car. With the Vitesse, Herald and Spitfire all having a large degree of commonality in mechanical design, fitting the new six-cylinder engine was a relatively easy matter, helped by the six-cylinder engine being comparatively short in length due to it being required to fit into the engine compartment of the Phase 3 Standard Vanguard, which had originally been designed to accommodate the four-cylinder wet-liner engine. With very similar designs, the Le Mans and Rally-prepared Spitfires are sometimes described as GT6s, but the Works Spitfires and the GT6 models were very different beasts. This confusion was exploited in period by Triumph, who promoted the new model as being developed from the race-winning Le Mans Spitfires.

GT6 Mk I

Triumph introduced their new fastback GT car as the GT6 in 1966. It bore similarities with the Spitfire Mk II then in production but with a power bulge fitted to the bonnet to accommodate the larger engine and a larger radiator fitted to deal with cooling. It shared its gearbox with the Vitesse, strengthened from the Spitfire product and now with synchromesh on all forward gears. An electrically operated and interlocked overdrive completed the transmission as an optional but very wise selection. This gave a 20 per cent advantage on third and top gear, providing effectively six forward gears. While overdrive third gear was the same ratio as normal top gear, it did provide a very useful facility for quickly changing between gears in urban environments. With the increased engine weight, stronger front springs were needed.

Below the waistline, the GT6 shared the same styling as the contemporary Spitfire, but at the rear an opening, glazed cover hatch was provided that was to promote many comments regarding similarity with Jaguar's E-Type fastback that used a similar design. And with the GT6 and its opening rear hatch and bonnet power bulge having such similarity to the Jaguar, it gained the name 'the poorer man's E-type'. It was, though, an entirely different car, addressing a different market.

An example of a rare Mk 1 GT6. The lack of an air vent in the metalwork behind the rear side windows confirms this is a Mk 1. (Joachim Kohler, CC BY-SA)

Inside, as an option, a small rear seat could be fitted, which was really only suitable for young children. The dashboard followed the style of the Spitfire Mk II and was given a wooden finish, but the side windows were modified with a forward-hinged quarterlight and the top of the drop glass re-profiled to fit the roofline. A heater and woollen carpets were a standard fitting, but the new car did meet some criticism for poor ventilation, especially in the warmer parts of North America. The ventilation issues were not unique to the GT6 as many smaller two-door saloon cars of the period also suffer from poor ventilation.

But while the car met with general approval, the handling issues of the Herald, which were also a characteristic of the Spitfire and Vitesse, became a serious problem with the heavier and more powerful GT6. Lifting-off power while cornering could provoke understeer in all models that used the same general suspension layout, but in the case of the GT6 and Vitesse, the large engine at the front certainly did not help matters. While drivers who understood the handling characteristics of the car and treated it with respect were not troubled, test reports in the motoring press, especially in the US where road safety had become an emotive issue, made a big issue of the handling and the reputation stuck.

Meanwhile, MG had developed their own GT version of their bestselling MGB model, powered using a twin-carburetted version of BMC's B series engine of 1800cc. Power delivery was broadly similar to the Triumph, but the Triumph, with the advantage of two extra cylinders, delivered the power more smoothly. Both cars had opening rear hatches, with the MG's similarly being hinged at the top. Model choice for the buyer ultimately came down to whether the buyer's allegiance sat with MG or Triumph.

GT6 Mk II

Triumph reacted rapidly to resolve the concerns over the handling with the announcement of the GT6 Mk II, known in North American markets as the GT6+. Launched for 1969, the new rear suspension design still utilised the basics of the Spitfire with the transverse leaf spring, but a cleverly designed lower wishbone was fitted between the car's rear chassis and the wheel hub carrier. Final drive shafts were now articulated by use of a 'Rotoflex' rubber doughnut coupling and the handling of the GT6 was now tamed. An increase in power to 105bhp was achieved with a revised cylinder head and modified cam settings, giving an advantage of around 10 per cent over the rival MGB GT. Visually, the changes were limited, with alterations to the front of the car where the front bumper was raised, as had been done with the Spitfire Mk III; cooling grilles were slotted into the front wings behind the front wheels; and vents were fitted to the rear quarter panel, providing for through-flow ventilation even with all the windows closed – a welcome improvement over the earlier car. Inside the cockpit, detail changes to the instrument dials saw the chrome rims replaced with matt black and toggle switches supplanted by rocker style. The requirements of legislation, either coming into force or anticipated, were also accommodated, with the new model now being fitted with dual-circuit braking.

Above: With the Mk II version of the GT6, cooling vents were added just behind the front wheels and, more importantly, behind the rear side windows to help with cabin ventilation.

Below: At the front, in line with changes made to the Spitfire, the front bumper height was raised. (Colin Radford)

Above: The cockpit of the GT6 was a comfortable place to be. Note the dashboard-mounted cooling vents. The three dials to the extreme left of the image are a more recent addition.

Below: The rear of this GT6 shows the 'hatchback' to good effect. In common with the Spitfire, the design was straightforward but effective.

GT6 Mk III

The Mk III and final version of the GT6 was launched at the end of 1970 and implemented the same general styling changes that were applied to the Spitfire Mk IV. Specifically, a new, de-seamed bonnet was fitted, in common with the Spitfire, and the rear-end design also adopted the cut-off style that was rapidly becoming a distinctive Triumph mark. There were no changes to the engine or transmission, but the improved aerodynamics increased the claimed top speed to 112mph and a 0–60mph time of 10 seconds. This comprehensively beat the rival MG MGB GT by 7mph in maximum speed and was 3 seconds faster to achieve 60mph, although the MG sold in larger numbers.

Sales continued as anticipated, but remained constrained as capacity was limited because of Heralds, Vitesses, Spitfires and GT6s all sharing the same assembly lines until the end of 1973, when the model was finally withdrawn from production. Suspension modifications came again earlier in 1973 with the adoption of the scheme used earlier for the Spitfire, with the leaf spring now on a pivot and a larger anti-roll bar fitted to the front. Further changes included the addition of a brake servo and cloth seats being fitted.

In common with the Spitfire, the Mk 3 GT6 benefitted from the new styling for the wings and bonnet assembly. The car is finished in magenta, a typical Triumph colour of the 1970s that many feel suits the GT6 particularly well.

Above: A rear view of a GT6 Mk 3 shows the redesigned rear that was to form a feature of most Triumph cars of the period. Bright yellows were also very popular in the 1970s.

Below: Finally, a GT6 participating in a club event and being driven with enthusiasm – as it was designed to be.

7

Petrol Injection TRs

Early in the life of the TR4 consideration had been given to utilising the maximum capacity possible using the wet-liner engine in a bid to extract even more power. A 90mm-diameter liner would give a capacity of 2341cc, which had originally been considered as a power plant for Standard-Triumph's commercial vehicle, the Atlas, soon to be built as part of the Leyland commercial vehicles label. Although providing a high-torque engine, it was considered to be inadequately refined for a delivery van, and certainly not suitable for a sports car. A maximum increase to 2,446cc, achieved through conversion to a dry-liner engine, was also contemplated, but this was equally unrefined and so to achieve more power than the TR4/4A product would require a different approach.

A possible solution could be with the six-cylinder engine that Triumph had been using with much success in the GT6, Vitesse and 2000 saloon models. The saloons were developing a reputation for performance in endurance rallying, where the 2-litre engine, fuelled through triple Weber carburettors and utilising a much modified cam profile, was developing in the region of 150bhp. Unfortunately, the levels of tuning required rendered the engine unsuitable for production use in a road car, but it did prove the levels of power that were possible from the engine. What was now needed was a method to develop that power with the level of refinement to meet the needs of the typical customer for a sports car using the car in normal traffic conditions. A primary consideration was whether the engine would fit under the bonnet; there were no great concerns as the six-cylinder engine had its origins in the final Standard Vanguard models earlier in the decade when a primary requirement for the new design was that it would fit the Vanguard's engine bay. Testing showed that it would equally well fit under a TR4A bonnet, but in normal tune the output of the six-cylinder engine was no more than was being produced by the existing four-cylinder engine in the TR4A.

At this time Triumph was interested in a new petrol-injection system, which had been developed initially by the aerospace arm of Lucas Industries. While ubiquitous now, petrol fuel injection in the mid-1960s was totally in the realm of extremely high-performance race cars or exotic models that were outside the price range of the typical Triumph customer. The advantages of a petrol-injection system were that it would provide exactly the right amount of fuel at the correct time, thus

Above: Seen from this angle, the body style differences between the TR4A and TR5 are subtle. The model badge, now offset, is the most obvious clue.

Below: There were few major differences in the cockpit between TR4A, TR5 and TR6. This image happens to be a TR5.

ensuring that the maximum power and efficiency could be extracted while producing minimal emissions, therefore having the dual benefit of solving the search for more performance and satisfying the requirement to minimise emissions, especially in the still important US market.

Fuel from the rear-mounted tank was fed through a filter to a high-pressure pump. The filter housing and the actual filters would be familiar to mechanics with knowledge of diesel systems, being of similar design and shape; however, the actual filters were different, and fitting a filter intended for use with diesel would cause it to rapidly break down and clog the system. The high-pressure pump then delivered fuel at a pressure of 106–110lbs sq in, maintained by an inline pressure-relief valve with excess fuel being returned to the filter. The high-pressure fuel pump was capable of a flow rate of 16 imperial gallons per hour, which was electrically powered by nothing more glamourous or sophisticated than a Lucas windscreen wiper motor. Despite its humble power source, the pump itself was a precision instrument with very tight manufacturing tolerances.

Changes under the bonnet were significant. A six-cylinder engine is now fuelled by Lucas Petrol Injection equipment. The throttle bodies and injectors are all visible in the foreground.

The now pressurised fuel was fed to the front of the car, where it entered a metering unit that supplied the fuel to the engine. The metering unit was powered by a control component driven mechanically from the engine's camshaft and controlled by a vacuum-operated unit that would permit the metering component to vary the amount of fuel to be delivered depending on the vacuum derived from the inlet manifold. Changes in vacuum determined the amount of power demanded and delivery accurately timed through its close connection to the distributor. Now pressurised, volume controlled and timed, the fuel was supplied to injectors, one per cylinder, mounted in three throttle bodies that were fitted to the engine in a similar manner as an inlet manifold and carburettors. Air was filtered and supplied through a large-volume plenum chamber and controlled by butterfly throttles, with each throttle body housing two such butterflies, effectively giving one throttle per cylinder.

Cold starting was facilitated through an excess fuel device that enriched the mixture, and idle speed was controlled initially by allowing a small amount of air leakage past the nominally closed butterflies. For the engine to run smoothly and efficiently, the synchronisation of the butterflies was crucial. To simplify matters, an early modification added a bleed valve to the front of the inlet balance pipe, so when idle the butterflies could be set at the closed position.

A close-up of a TR5 shows the front anti-roll bar and enamel TR5 badge. This example has been fitted with lightweight 'Minilite' wheels.

Badging was minimalist, with just the TR5 badge fitted.

In parallel with the petrol-injection system development, Triumph's engine developers had increased the stroke to 95mm, giving a total capacity of 2,498cc. With this capacity, the fuel injection and a suitable cam, the engine was capable of producing 150bhp and was deemed to meet the requirements for the new model.

Unfortunately, while the power requirement was met, the control over emissions was a different matter. It was quickly realised that the Lucas petrol-injection system as implemented in the TR5 could not reliably meet the emissions standards present in the United States; therefore, an alternative solution would be required for that market. The solution for the US was simple: twin Zenith-Stromberg carburettors would supply the fuel mixture and the model, with unique badges and model name, would be known as a TR250.

While the new engine provided the bulk of the changes, there were also a number of other mechanical enhancements. An alternator replaced the earlier dynamo, and a vacuum servo was now considered to be a necessity. The bonnet badge location was offset and took the form of an enamelled trapezoidal shape, displaying either TR 5 or TR 250 as appropriate, and a badge denoting '2500' was fitted to the rear wing, along with side marker lights. TR250 models also gained a highly distinctive transverse 'racing stripe' across the bonnet and down the wings.

Even during the genesis of the TR5, serious consideration was given to the model to follow the TR5. In the late 1960s the British motor industry was in a state of turmoil.

Above: Triumph had decided that the PI system would not meet US emissions regulations, therefore cars destined for North America were equipped with traditional twin carburettors. These cars were designated TR250 with a different bonnet badge and 'racing stripes' fitted as standard.

Below: All TR250s were built as left-hand drive, although some have been converted to right-hand drive. Other than the modern door mirrors, this is a good example of a TR250 in as-built condition with Surrey roof.

Vauxhall Motors had long been absorbed into the General Motors combine, along with Opel of Germany, and some commonality in their product offering was becoming more apparent. The Rootes organisation had grown from their acquisition of smaller companies over the years. Masters of the art of badge engineering, the Rootes Group would soon be bought outright by Chrysler. Ford were large enough to continue on their own and were rapidly dominating the market share in the UK. Meanwhile, the two largest motor groups in the UK were BMC, formed in the early 1950s with a merger of the Nuffield Group with Austin, and Leyland Motors, whose strength came from their highly successful truck and bus business, along with their car interest in Triumph.

The TR5 replacement – called, naturally, TR6 – marked a move away from Italian styling. Michelotti had gained a formidable reputation for his ability and, being much in demand, was unable to provide his flair to Triumph for the new TR6, even though he continued to work for Leyland designing cabs for their lorries and would eventually design the Leyland National bus that would become a familiar sight on UK streets.

Instead, the project was given to Karmann of Germany, whose brief was to revise the front and rear of the car but, other than a few detail changes, leave the centre section

Finished in Sapphire Blue, the TR6 shown here shows the modifications made to the front of the car by Karmann.

With the roof lowered, the TR6 still retains all the essential style of the earlier cars. This car was previously owned by the author and, despite TR6 PIs having a reputation for unreliability, was used for many long-distance touring holidays without serious incident.

alone. This was following much the same strategy as had earlier seen the successful transformation of the Spitfire through its own iterations. At the rear, the car was given a flat boot lid, leading to a cut-off, vertical tail finished in a satin black colour, while the front was also squared off and the headlights moved to the outer extremities. With this new, squared-off appearance the side and indicator lamps were repositioned to the front of the car, with a wing-mounted repeater for turn signals. On the earliest builds, the windscreen surround was finished in body colour, but this was soon changed to a satin black finish. As a consequence of the new TR being styled by Karmann, the commonality of style that was being established across all Triumph models was not extended to the TR6.

As an option, a conventional hard top finished in body colour replaced the surrey top that had been available with the TR4, 4A and 5, and the car could be ordered as a fixed head or a convertible with the hard top available as an accessory. It was possible to fit the hard top without completely removing the hood as the same windscreen mounting points as the soft top were used, while at the rear the soft top securing bolts were similarly used.

Mechanically, the car remained little changed, with the same engines and transmission as the TR5. Instead of creating a bespoke model for the US, where the petrol-injection models still could not be sold due to the challenges of meeting the ever-tightening emissions regulations, the US model was known simply as TR6. Injection-powered models wore a badge below the Triumph emblem at the rear of the car proclaiming their injected status; this was omitted on US models. The injected motor still developed a claimed 150bhp, while the US model needed to make do with just 106bhp.

For the TR6, Triumph returned to the traditional removable hard top as seen here. The rear end styling can also be clearly seen.

Changes came in 1972, with modifications primarily to the injection system and the fitting of a revised camshaft, said to make the car more drivable in town traffic. Coupled with a change in the measurement parameters, the stated output of the PI engine was decreased to 125bhp with no change to the US models. For the US, compliance dictated the fitting of new seats with high backs and integral headrests and the raising of bumper heights. This required the front lights to be relocated, along with revisions to the mounting points for the bumpers. The scuttle-mounted opening air vent, which had been a feature of all TRs from the very beginning, was replaced with a plastic grille and the instruments were now finished with a matt black rim rather than the chrome finish used earlier. Similarly, wiper arms were now plated in matt black due to a combination of fashion changes and a claim to improve road safety by reducing dazzle. Finally, a revised overdrive was fitted that now operated only on third and top gear.

The petrol-injection system was gaining a reputation for unreliability, made worse with the changes introduced in 1972. While the earlier system used a linkage that synchronised all the butterfly throttle, the new system split the mechanism into three, with the first section operating the second, and the second operating the third. With wear in the system, keeping the throttles synchronised became more difficult. Further problems arose from the need to maintain a high-pressure fuel supply: the degree of accuracy and cleanliness needed in setting up the injection components, coupled with the need for the engine to be in good order,

Above: Under the bonnet, there was little change from the TR5 to TR6. Note that a second bonnet-release mechanism has been fitted, a common improvement as the primary release system was known to be a problem area that could result in drastic action being required should it fail.

Below: TR6s also gained a steering lock during production, with the ignition lock being positioned beneath the steering column. Early TR6 models had secondary instruments with needles that hung down, while later models had these dials with upwards-facing needles. The steering wheel is an aftermarket item and the door cappings have been changed to match the dashboard.

developing a strong vacuum for the metering unit to function as intended and a good electrical supply to the high-pressure fuel pump being essential to maintain the fuel pressure. With the typical garage of the time being more familiar with setting up and balancing multiple carburettors and a lack of training, the PI system was frequently replaced with a simpler twin-carburettor system – a situation that was shared with Triumph's flagship saloon car, the 2.5PI. However, modern cherished classic models that are set up as intended by Lucas have shown that the system will meet the design requirements of more power with lower emissions.

The motoring press were generally impressed with both the TR5 and TR6, with the TR6 gaining the epithet as 'the last of the hairy chested sports cars'. During the long lifetime of the TR6, a major reorganisation of the largest indigenous British motor manufacturers occurred that commentators have marked as being the beginning of the decline of the British motor industry. First, Jaguar had expanded with the absorption of the British Daimler company (not to be confused with the German company of the same name that produces Mercedes-Benz models) and then Guy Motors, a truck and bus manufacturer that rivalled Leyland but which had found itself in receivership as a result of a number of poor business decisions. The now enlarged Jaguar company then agreed terms to merge with BMC to form the short-lived British Motor Holdings. Then, finally, with encouragement by the government at the time, British Motor Holdings merged with Leyland Motors to form British Leyland. This resulted in a shuffling of personnel and, significantly for Triumph, Harry Webster, who had been involved with the engineering of the TR range from the very beginning, now moved to the volume car division. Industrial unrest grew, resulting in a material fall in product quality, extended delivery times and a lack of investment for new models. Management were distracted by constant reorganisations, with key staff being moved between divisions, and funding for new models was all but non-existent. This all manifested itself with the review of a new TR6 that was supplied to the editor of the influential magazine *Motor Sport*. The conclusion of the article described the car as having 'so many faults that it might well have been the first car off the production line of a new model' and 'its general finish was appalling, mechanically it was dreadful, and it was to be another 5,500 miles before this Lucas fuel-injected motor car was to run consistently on six cylinders'.

Nevertheless, at the time that the TR6 finally closed the door on separate chassis TRs, production was close to 95,000 models and the cars remained very popular in export markets, with around 90 per cent sold outside of the home market.

TR6 Competition Cars

Despite the successes of the similarly powered Triumph 2.5PI and 2500PI models in endurance racing, especially the 1970 World Cup Rally from London to Mexico, the injected TRs did not form part of the works' motor sport efforts. Triple Weber-fuelled TR6s did have success in circuit and endurance racing in North America, especially those prepared by Group 44, sponsored by the official distributors of Triumph products in North America. Well-known film star Paul Newman had a strong interest in motor sport and won the US National Championship SCCA in 1976 driving a TR6. Privately entered TR6 cars have continued to be used in classic racing events and club events.

8

Triumph Stag

The most expensive Triumph model came about by an unusual alignment of ideas by Michelotti and Triumph. Following the successful launch of the 2000 saloon in 1963, thoughts quickly turned to a facelift model to be launched later in the decade, while at the same time Michelotti had some ideas of his own to produce a Grand Touring car that would offer true competition to the Mercedes SL. Following discussions with Harry Webster, Director of Engineering, a Triumph 2000 was shipped to Italy, and a new prototype quickly emerged. Using a shortened wheelbase, the front of the car was cut square with a slatted grille, sidelight and turn indicators were fitted to the sides of the grille (one above the other) and the squared-off appearance was applied at the rear. The arrangement between Webster and Michelotti was that if Triumph liked the prototype they had first refusal. Triumph immediately liked what was on offer, with production development swiftly put in place with some secrecy, meaning that Michelotti's plan to use the prototype as an example of his craft was not to be. As was usual with Triumph development practice, the new model was given a four-letter development code – in this case, 'STAG'.

From the supplied Triumph 2000, the front suspension was based on struts and the rear used a similar semi-trailing arm system, as originally conceived for the TR4A. The front and rear aspects provided the inspiration for the Triumph house style that emerged, particularly the rear styling of later Spitfires and GT6s, the Mk II Triumph 2000 and 2500 big saloon and later Dolomite mid-size saloons as well as the Stag.

Engine power for the prototype initially came from the six-cylinder engine used in the GT6 and saloon and for production, though the enlarged 2,500cc engine used in the TR250 was considered. However, since the time of the Leyland Motors takeover, Triumph had been working in the background on a range of modular engines to supplant the four-cylinder SC engine used in the Spitfire and its associated six-cylinder derivative, both of which owed their original to the engine developed to power the Standard 8 of the early 1950s. A design requirement for the new engine programme was to develop a range of new engines that would be suitable to fulfil the needs of the company well into the 1970s. A prime objective of this exercise had been to create a range of engines, from an inline four through to a range-topping V8, based on common components and

Under the bonnet, the V8 engine of the Stag.

manufacturing tools, thus simplifying manufacturing and training for the Triumph dealer service network. The addition of the Lucas petrol-injection system was seen as a benefit to maximise power and allow emerging and foreseeable future emission standards to be met. The PI system was quickly abandoned and instead fuel delivery was left to Stromberg carburettors, with the engine capacity enlarged to 3 litres. In this configuration, the engine developed an advertised 145bhp, measured using the DIN standard, although the addition of pollution-control equipment for models bound for North America reduced the engine output to 127bhp.

The SAAB Connection

Triumph maintained a consultancy agreement with the engineering firm of Ricardo, who coincidentally had been retained by the Swedish company of SAAB to design a new engine. SAAB were intending to replace their existing Ford-sourced V4 engine – which itself had replaced a three-cylinder, two-stroke motor – with a new engine to be announced in the forthcoming SAAB 99 saloon. Ricardo quickly observed the closeness of Triumph's design thoughts with SAAB's needs, especially the need for the engine to be of about 1,500cc, four cylinders in line, suitable for front-wheel-drive applications and low in profile. With the Triumph family of engines being designed to be capable of being built in both straight- and V-format engines, the slant-engine format was an immediate benefit of it being 'half a V8'.

Triumph and SAAB were introduced to one another, and the first application of the new Triumph engine was as a power plant for the new SAAB. SAAB ultimately licensed production themselves and made various detail designs as their own model range expanded. One seemingly unimportant feature of the SAAB requirements for front-wheel drive dictated that the water pump for the engine would need to be mounted on top of the engine driven off the camshaft, rather than belt driven at the front of the engine in line with common practice of the era. This placed the head of the coolant system above the level of the radiator and required extra care when checking and adding coolant to ensure that the pump was pumping liquid and not sat in an airlock. The engine block itself was traditionally cast in iron, with the heads being in an aluminium alloy and the overhead cam driven by a simplex chain.

For the body design, Triumph remained true to Michelotti's original design, retaining the long, flat bonnet and luggage compartment. The trademark Michelotti 'shoulder' that

Often considered one of the more ergonomic dashboard designs of the era, the interior of the Stag shares much design language with Triumph's contemporary saloon cars. Notice the overdrive switch fitted to the centre of the gear change, a distinctive feature of many Triumphs.

was so distinctive a feature on all his sports car designs for Triumph was retained, but flattened a little and positioned further behind the doors than it was on the TR models and, in recognition with anticipated legislation changes in the US, a T-shaped roll bar was fitted just behind the doors and centrally at the top of the windscreen frame. The roll bar had another advantage in adding additional stiffness to the car. The cockpit was a true four-seater and trimmed to a more luxurious level than other Triumphs of the period, with electric windows, a full set of instruments set in a wooden dashboard and a hinged cover to neatly retain the folding roof when lowered. A traditional steel hard top was also available, either as a separate option or with changes to the product pricing, sometimes included with the base price car.

Automatic transmission based on a Borg-Warner unit was an option that was frequently selected in keeping with the car's status; otherwise, Triumph fitted the usual four-speed transmission with overdrive on third and top gear and standard-fit power steering made the car light and easy to drive.

Originally intended to be launched during 1968, the car finally hit the market two years late and was launched as a unique example of a car using its production code as its model name. The market welcomed this new range-topping Triumph model with great exultation, and a long waiting list rapidly grew for new models. It was priced below its most obvious rival, the Mercedes SL, but manufacturing costs were high, not helped by the engine

Wearing its hard top and with the 'Sundym' glass obvious in the light, the overall appearance of the Stag was very attractive. Triumph were again innovators in fitting light alloy wheels as a standard feature on cars.

being unique to the model and not shared in V8 format with the any of the model range. And perhaps Triumph, now being enmeshed in the disaster that was surrounding British Leyland at the time quickly lost its quality reputation along with not possessing the cachet or exclusivity of the alternative marques.

Overheating Issues

Launched with great fanfare in the United States, intended to be its prime market, it was again to sell well initially, but very quickly in both the US and home market the car gained a reputation for unreliability – particularly the engine, and especially problems that were caused by overheating. The care required in filling the coolant system (described previously) became more apparent in the Stag installation, especially when used in traffic or hot climates, where coolant would normally be ejected into an expansion vessel. There was a risk of it not being drawn back if air was present in the cooling circuit once the engine cooled. Overheating engines caused a higher than expected number of head gasket failures, which if not repaired urgently would result in the head becoming warped, leading to expensive repairs. Cars would be returned to owners with the head gasket issue resolved, but often without the root cause of the overheating problem being addressed. None of this was helped by the radiator itself being of marginal performance and there were numerous reports in the motoring press describing how significant amounts of casting sand had been found in the waterways.

To make matters even worse, the use of an iron block and alloy head made the use of anticorrosion additives in the cooling system absolutely essential. Just topping up with water or sub-standard anti-freeze mixture would cause electrolytic corrosion between the iron and alloy, with the resulting sediment precipitating in the radiator and thus reducing its efficiency even further. It must be remembered that the mixed use of iron and alloys in engines was not common in cars of the era, and in the case of Triumph, unique to this engine; therefore, it can be understood how the average owner or garage attendant would not be aware of the importance of using the correct antifreeze, unlike today. Low-compression pistons and advanced ignition timing to meet the tightening US legislation caused the engines to run even hotter, and the US option of air conditioning did nothing to help the situation.

As if that was not enough of a problem, the overhead cam on each bank of the engine was driven by a simplex chain that was found to stretch and, in extremis, jump a tooth or two, resulting in mistimed valve events, with the end result being contact between valve and piston and consequently a wrecked engine. Certainly, in the UK each dealer would only sell a small number of Stags. As a result, while they would see the many problems that affected the model, it was unlikely that they would see enough cars through the workshop to recognise a pattern. Removing the cylinder heads could also be difficult as a clever feature of the design, intended to simplify manufacturing, was to have half of the cylinder head fixings securing vertically into the block, while the remainder were angled. Unfortunately, this, with uneven heating and stresses in the engine, could cause problems in removing the head.

Whether the many problems of the time could have been resolved with greater production remains a question. Triumph had plans to use the V8 engine in a final revision to its large saloon range, but these never came to fruition, at least not as factory-produced cars. A small number of 'Stag Saloons' and 'Stag Estates' were produced by Atlantic Garages, a Triumph dealer in the west of England.

Alternative Power Sources

Many desperate owners looked for alternative power sources for their cars, with the 2,500cc straight six Triumph engine being a popular choice, along with Ford V6 engines and, not surprisingly, the Rover V8 3,500cc engine that many claim should have been the power plant of choice for the Stag. The reason that it was not comes down to a few simple facts: during the early design phase for the Stag the engine was not available; once Rover were absorbed into BL, production capacity was insufficient to provide the number of engines to fulfil the growing need for Rover and Range Rover production; and with the difference in engine weights, a redesign of the front suspension would have been necessary. Triumph had faith in their own product and many cherished cars have the various original manufacturing shortcomings resolved through improved cooling systems. Larger radiators, meticulously careful rebuilds and stronger timing chains bear witness to this, with Triumph Stags having a strong following by enthusiasts and a high survival rate. On top of everything, the Triumph V8 engine has an unmistakable soundtrack all of its own.

Model Revisions

Rather than adopt the traditional Triumph nomenclature of mark revision, the Stag was instead updated through factory-build sanctions, with minor revisions coinciding with model year changes to keep the car appearing fresh in buyer's minds. An early mechanical revision saw the cooling system pressure increased, giving a higher boiling point in an attempt to cure the overheating issue. The first recognisable change occurred for the 1973 model year when the coachwork was enhanced with a twin coachline. The sills were also painted with a satin black finish. A subtle change in the cabin saw the needles in the smaller instrument gauges changed from pointing upwards to pointing downwards. A slightly smaller steering wheel was also fitted as standard, and the design of the front seats was modified to allow headrests to be fitted. Headrests would quickly change from being an optional extra to a standard factory fit.

For 1976, the sills reverted to body colour, with a stainless-steel cover being fitted on models destined for the US market, although this rapidly became a standard fitting on all cars. Keeping pace with US safety requirements required detail lighting changes, emission-control systems and reinforcing bars in the doors to increase safety in the event of a side collision.

Above: More familiarly seen with the hard top removed and the folding soft top stowed under its cover, this Stag is seen on a club-organised event. The 'Rostyle' wheel trims are as originally fitted.

Below: With the folding roof erected, the frontal image with twin headlights shared many similarities with the 2000/2500 executive saloons of the period.

Above: The rear view of the Stag – again, with the roof raised – shows the tail design that was common across many Triumph models.

Below and opposite: A look at something that might have been had Triumph and British Leyland not been in such parlous conditions at the time – Michelotti's prototype for a fastback Stag.

Triumph also revised the wheel trims during production, in keeping with current fashion. Initially, cars were delivered with a wheel trim emulating a Rostyle wheel type. Despite the road wheels being secured by four bolts, the Rostyle trims created an impression of a five-bolt fitting. Wire wheels were offered for the US market initially, later to be replaced with a five-spoke alloy wheel from 1973 onwards and as an option elsewhere until 1976 when the alloys became the standard fitting.

Production ended in 1978 and was not replaced, although several alternatives had been considered. One, designed by Michelotti, contemplated a GT6-inspired fastback, with one example known to exist of the three originally built. Finally, a couple of design studies were undertaken on a TR7/TR8 theme, with prototypes being built but cancelled at an early stage.

9

TR7 and TR8 – The Wedge

As a result of the mergers that created British Leyland, Triumph found themselves united with old adversaries. Rover, who introduced their P6 2000 model at the same time as Triumph's own 2000 saloon, were now part of the same group, having been purchased by Leyland Motors in 1967, as were arch sports car rival MG. Clearly some form of model consolidation was inevitable and made economic sense, even if the rival groups of enthusiasts were not so certain. Triumph had lost the services of long-term engineering chief Harry Webster, who had been transferred to assist in the volume car division where there was a desperate need to get new models into production. Webster was replaced by Spen King, an equally distinguished engineer who had previously worked at Rover as Chief Engineer in charge of new vehicle projects, which included the P6 saloon car.

Triumph found themselves in the 'specialist car' division of BL, along with Rover and Jaguar. The sensible approach was for Jaguar to service the top end of the market, both for large saloons and sports cars; Rover and Triumph would attack the mid-range, mid-price market for saloon cars; and Triumph, along with MG, would service the sports car market, sitting beneath Jaguar.

The Leyland Corporate Sports Car

While planning for the car to replace both the TR6 and MGB, a wide-ranging review of market needs and design trends was undertaken. The volume division of British Leyland, comprising predominantly Austin and Morris, had a strong reputation for innovation, especially in terms of transverse engine layout, front-wheel drive and sophisticated suspension systems. This technology might fit well into the emerging market for mid-engined sports cars, but a research visit to the dealer network in the still important US market undertaken by Spen King and Mike Carver from the product planning department suggested otherwise. As a result of this research, it became very clear that the US market for sports cars still required competitively priced cars that would compete with the growing flow of Japanese sports cars employing fundamentally straightforward engineering that was easy to maintain. This ruled out the more advanced mid-engined, hydrolastic suspended models that might otherwise have been considered and pointed to a simpler front-engine, rear-wheel-driven car following the template of both the earlier TRs and the MGB.

For simplicity of production, it was seen as important that the requirements of the US regarding safety were employed as standard and not as product revisions, as had happened to both the TR6 and MGB during their product life. Of great concern was a well-held belief that new open-top cars were about to be banned in the US in the pursuit of greater road safety. Such regulations never actually manifested but were sufficient to convince British Leyland that the new TR, and indeed the replacement for the highly acclaimed Jaguar E-Type, would need to be closed-topped coupés.

Mechanically, the new car would be powered by existing engines from within the company's portfolio. For the volume market, a 2-litre version of the slant-four engine that had originally been supplied to SAAB and which formed 'half a Stag' engine was the obvious choice. It had a high power capability and the slant format provided for a

An original, unmolested Speke-built TR7. Note the flat centre section of the bonnet.

low, downward-sloping bonnet line. At the high end, the model would offer V8 power. The decision was whether this should be the Triumph or Rover product. The Triumph option would have been the 3-litre engine used in the Stag and considered as a potential range-topping product for the envisaged Mk III version of the 'big six' Triumph saloon that was never built; the Rover engine, an alloy engine of 3,500cc capacity and originally designed by Buick, was familiar from its use in Rover's P5B and P6B saloon models and Range Rover. With concerns over warranty claims from Stag owners and negative sentiment about the Triumph engine in the motoring press, the choice was made: the Rover engine would be used. Sitting in between, a higher-performance version of the 2-litre engine was pencilled in. This engine was essentially the slant-four engine, but with a modified valve arrangement such that a sixteen-valve cylinder head could be implemented using a single overhead cam and was also used in the Dolomite Sprite Saloon. This valve arrangement was another 'first' for Triumph, winning an industry award for innovation. Essentially, the overhead cam sat above and operated the usual inlet and exhaust valves, but an additional set of rockers operated a second set of valves, giving the power increase of a sixteen-valve engine but without the complexity of twin camshafts. In production format, the engine developed 127bhp but had the capability in motor sport tuning to provide substantially more – in the region of 150bhp.

Transmission was originally a four speed without the option of overdrive, but the most significant change to the car's layout was the suspension. Gone was the semi-trailing arm independent rear suspension, now replaced with a beam axle with coil springs, radius arms and, at last, telescopic dampers. At the front, the suspension was based on MacPherson struts. Spen King was firmly of the opinion that a well-designed and specified beam-axle suspension system was both simpler, cheaper and lighter in weight than an indifferent independent system – not that Triumph's independent suspension system, as implemented first in the 2000 saloon, Stag and more recent TRs, was in any way indifferent.

That Wedge Design...

Body styling was, as usual for Triumph models, initially outsourced to Michelotti, but with changing times, was rejected by management. A revolutionary design by in-house stylist Harris Mann, however, did meet with approval. Mann was working in the volume car division following a period at Ford of Europe where he had worked on Ford's much-appreciated Capri coupé, and was strongly in favour of a distinctive 'wedge' design of cars for the late 1970s and 1980s. Mann was also responsible for the Austin Allegro, originally designed as another wedge style but drastically changed for production, and the Leyland 18-22 Princess series of large saloons. Any thoughts of building on a theme of continuous evolution through the TR range were completely abandoned with the new striking wedge design. With its unmistakable wedge shape, short rear overhang and swooping side swage lines, it received enormous amounts of criticism at the time.

As the front profile was not of the type that would accommodate traditional headlights, the solution was to fit pop-up ones that folded completely into the front apron. In much the same way that the petrol-injection system fuel pump was powered by the ubiquitous

Above: Viewed from the rear, the wedge shape is more noticeable, and the scalloped sides are very apparent.

Below: With the headlights illuminated, the reason for the pop-up lights is obvious as the frontal design could not accommodate fixed lamps.

The interior of the TR7 was a well-furnished and comfortable place to be for a sports car.

Lucas windscreen wiper motor, that same basic windscreen wiper motor was used to operate the pop-up function of the headlights. The very low front profile of the car gave rise to a comment in several published road tests that the front of the car could not be seen as it sat far below the driver's sight line. This was also a concern when the car was used in rallying as accurate positioning of the car could be critical and resulted in the lights being fixed in an 'up' position for the cars prepared for motor sport. The car also utilised an early implementation of printed wiring for the dashboard, switches and instruments. The cabin was comfortably furnished, with seats covered in a bright tartan finish. It was as different to the preceding TR6 as could be imagined, but as Spen King was reputed to have commented, it returned the TR to its origins – an affordable, 2-litre-powered car with a live axle.

First Production

The new car was first launched in January 1975, with all production initially being designated for the US. TR7s were built at Triumph's factories in Speke on Merseyside, a facility that had existed for some years pressing bodies for Triumph and latterly building complete cars. Engines were built at Canley on the outskirts of Coventry and transported northwards for assembly. Production for other markets was promised for later in 1975, but it was well into 1976 before deliveries actually commenced. As all cars produced were

Above: Another car from early in the production run, finished in what appears to be an unusual colour for a sports car, but shades of brown were very fashionable in the 1970s.

Below: With the move of production to Canley, the TR7 decal gave way to the Triumph circular laurel emblem as seen here. Finished in Persian Aqua metallic and fitted with the later V8-accommodating bonnet, this particular car has the highly desirable full-length sunroof.

equipped with just a four-speed transmission, the car was described as being under geared, making long distances tiring as a result of the high engine speed. Otherwise, the cabin was very comfortable, especially when compared with the traditionally built body on chassis set-up of the earlier TR cars. Triumph did have a suitable overdrive implementation from the Dolomite saloon range available but had chosen not to offer it. Perhaps the reason for the omission of an overdrive was the increased availability of five-speed transmissions and a thought that an overdrive was consequently becoming anachronistic, although the four-cylinder factory-prepared TR7s for rallying did include overdrive. Some drivers familiar with earlier TRs also commented on the poor braking efficiency, despite the continued use of servo-assisted discs at the front. The absence of an open TR was lamented by many owners, but the car could be fitted with a full-length folding sunroof, which when fully opened provided a close approximation to an open car.

A five-speed gearbox and a strengthened rear axle was soon offered, based on a design for the new Rover 3500 SD1, which was to be widely used throughout the BL product range. This followed the option of an automatic transmission in 1976 – an option that was rarely specified even in the US. The new five-speed gearbox became a standard item on US cars and an option elsewhere as soon as it was available. However, production shortages quickly led to the new gearbox being reserved for US-bound models until 1978 when it became a standard across all markets.

Production of the new TR7 was to suffer as a result of circumstances, some of which were outside the control of the company. The 1970s oil crisis was to have a profound effect on all motor manufacturers, and the new British Leyland business suffered badly. The end result of numerous long-established manufacturing businesses that had been thrown together in forming British Leyland provided overlapping product ranges, competing factories and often dealers who were in direct competition with other dealers in the same geographic area now selling essentially the same product range. Industrial relations throughout the motor industry had been difficult for many years and the lack of investment or modernisation did not help. Inevitably, British Leyland teetered on the verge of bankruptcy and looked to the government for help. The result was nationalisation. A comprehensive review of operations might have helped, but it did not. Strikes at the Speke plant, some over the most trivial of issues, became common, leading to delays in production. Rumours circulated about closure, leading to reduced morale within the workforce.

More Performance

TR7 production continued in the background to all of this and plans to introduce a higher-performance car were reviewed. Following the naming convention of the Dolomite, the higher-performance version of the TR7 utilising the sixteen-valve engine was intended to be marketed as the TR7 Sprint. Prototypes were built and tested, and the performance increase was noticeable. The standard engine produced 105bhp in non-Federal form, but the Sprint engine was capable of 127bhp in production form, with the original versions of the Dolomite Sprint easily capable of 135bhp until it was decided to derate the engine to simplify production.

All this came to an end on 1 November 1977, when the entire workforce at Speke walked out on strike. On the very same day, a new government-appointed chairman of British Leyland took office. New chairman Sir Michael Edwardes was to stand for no nonsense, and with the TR selling at a loss, there was no hurry on management's behalf to settle the strike. In February 1978, the board took the decision to close the Speke plant in its entirety. Despite commentators considering that such an action would provoke an all-out strike across all Leyland plants and likely spread to the entire car industry, the workforce, bowing to the inevitable, accepted the closure plans, with the final car coming off the line in May 1978.

Relocation to the Midlands

With Triumph being something of a 'halo' brand that enticed customers into BL showrooms, the decision was made to relocate production elsewhere and so body pressings were to be formed at Pressed Steel in Swindon, another BL Group company, and assembly would be at Standard-Triumph's spiritual home at Canley. The first Canley-produced car came off the line in the autumn of 1978.

The most apparent change to the cars could be seen at the front, where the Triumph laurel wreath replaced the previous TR7 decals. Production only continued at Canley for two years when the decision was made to close the Canley works for production entirely, resulting in TR7 production being moved once again, this time to the Rover plant in

After the final move of production to Solihull, another new badge was fitted. This example, finished in Cavalry Blue, also has the full-length sunroof.

Solihull. Once again, the front logo was changed to a circular-applied badge. The change of badging with each move does provide an easy way to quickly identify the manufacturing plant that a car was built. The later Solihull-built cars are often considered the best quality.

One significant victim of the turmoil would be the TR7 Sprint programme, which was quietly abandoned once the move from Speke took place. A small number of pre-production TR7 Sprints were sold, all fixed-head coupés, primarily to people with close contacts with the company. These can be identified by the TR7 Sprint badge at the front.

Above and left: The TR7 that never made it to production. Badged as a TR7 Sprint, this is one of a small number of genuine, factory-built Sprint cars to have escaped the usual fate reserved for prototypes.

With the conversion being a relatively simple matter of replacing the existing engine with that intended for, or taken from a Dolomite Sprint, several owners have undertaken the conversion themselves, ideally with a five-speed transmission and uprated brakes.

The Convertible Arrives

Once it had become clear that the threatened US ban on open-top cars was not going to materialise, plans were put in place to create a convertible version of the car. This time the styling was undertaken by Michelotti and based on the existing coupé, which resulted in an attractive design that, from any angle, looks as though the car had been originally conceived as an open car and not converted from the original. Ten convertible prototypes had been built at Speke prior to the shutdown in spring 1978, but it was to be a year before the cars went on general sale, and then only in the US market. There was a further year's delay until March 1980 before the 'new' model, now described as the TR7 Drophead, went on general sale in all markets. The convertible met a good reception from the press, with numerous comments suggesting that it was the car that the TR7 always should have been.

Still retaining the wedge shape below the window line, the convertible TR7 looks to be an entirely different car.

TR7 V8

The other project that had survived the move from Merseyside to the Midlands was the V8-powered car. Initially developed for competition use by the motor sport department that was based at the MG plant in Abingdon, the first implementation of the Rover V8 engine was in April 1978 and given the description of TR7 V8. To allow the cars to compete, the team at Abingdon needed to convince the governing bodies of motor sport that 400 such cars had been built. The primary application of the TR7 V8 was in rallying, where it had some success and replaced the earlier TR7 models that utilised the sixteen-valve Sprint engine.

TR7 Sprints and TR7 V8s did have a period of success in rallying, driven by names such as Tony Pond, Brian Culcheth, Roger Clark and Scandinavian drivers Per Eklund and Simo Lampinen. In an interview with the author, Brian Culcheth expressed his disappointment with the TR7, noting that it was very difficult to see the front corners of the car, making it difficult to position the car accurately, and there was wayward handling, describing it in testing: 'These cars had poor steering as well. You could go round the same turn six times without any problem, but on the seventh for no good reason, it would just run off the

Originally driven by Simo Lampinen and showing off its British Airways sponsorship livery, TR7 V8s, including this example, had much success.

road. Especially when testing, there were sections of "off" that I got quite familiar with!' Brian, of course, had a long period of rally driving for Triumph, initially in the TR4 and most famously in the 1970 London to Mexico World Cup Rally where he was to finish in a Triumph 2.5PI saloon a close second to Hannu Mikkola's Ford Escort before continuing with the TR7 rally cars.

TR8 Introduced

Prior to the move to Canley, a batch of pre-production V8-powered cars were assembled at Speke during 1977. To accommodate the engine, it had been found necessary to incorporate a central bulge in the bonnet, so to rationalise production all TR7 models produced subsequently would feature the additional bonnet bulge. The new TR8 was announced in the US market during the summer of 1979, initially as a coupé but with convertibles available later in the year. The only visual differences between the TR7 and TR8 were badges and wider tyres.

Timing for British Leyland could not have been worse. Just as the TR8 was introduced, the US market, which had long been the spiritual home of the gas-guzzling V8-powered car, was transitioning to an era of smaller, more economical models – at least by US terms – as a result of continual increases in the cost of oil and the general economic malaise of the time. Press reception was very mixed, with many comments of wallowing suspension, poor handling and tyre squeal when cornering with enthusiasm. The mandatory US emission-control equipment limited the power output of the car to just 133bhp – only slightly more than the power capability of the Sprint engine in production, originally planned as an option for the TR7. For Californian models, where emission controls were even stricter, Triumph introduced an electronically controlled fuel-injection system manufactured by Lucas under licence from Bosch and based on the latter's L-Jetronic system. This could then manage to deliver 137bhp. Transmission options were either a five-speed manual or a Borg-Warner Type 65 three-speed automatic.

Fate was not kind to the TR8 and so very few genuine examples exist. This one is known to be a genuine, factory-built TR8. Visual differences were minimal – just TR8 badges in place of TR7 and wider tyres.

Under the bonnet of a TR8 could be found the Rover 3,500cc V8, originally designed in the US by Buick. Again, this is a genuine factory-built car.

The TR8 was never sold officially through dealers in any market except the United States, although a pre-production run of sixty-three coupés and eighteen convertibles for the domestic market had been built. Some of these were factory registered and eventually resold. Sadly, the market for large-capacity V8-powered compact sports cars was coming to an end, just at the time that Triumph was getting the TR8 ready for production. With car sales in the US continuing to create a financial loss on each car sold, it was inevitable that harsh financial reality would eventually result in the end of production.

An advantage of the car being engineered to accept the Rover V8 engine means it has been a relatively simple task to replace a TR7 with a V8, along with uprating suspension, transmission and braking, to produce what is in effect an 'aftermarket' TR8. In particular, Grinnal had much success uprating TR7s to V8 specification and, with subtle modifications to the bodywork, produced what might have been a facelifted version of the TR8 – had production continued.

October 1981 saw the final TR7 roll off the production line. It was a silver/bronze-coloured convertible. It had become something of a tradition to save the final example of most models for posterity, so this car now resides in the collection of the British Motor Museum at Gaydon in Warwickshire. It brought an end to the production of Triumph sports cars which had commenced in the late 1920s and had sold in good numbers, establishing a solid reputation for the company.

Had things been different, this might have been the most sought-after Wedge – a TR8 convertible. The car is badged as having a 3.5-litre engine, but the owner could not be found to confirm its history. The badge suggests it is a car from the Solihull era.

Will there be a new Triumph sports car? When BMW disposed of their ownership of Rover Group, the final incarnation of what had been British Leyland, many of the brand names were similarly disposed of. The exception being Riley and Triumph, whose brand names remain the property of BMW AG. From time to time, teaser articles appear in the motoring press, but as of 2025 nothing other than design ideas have appeared, many created by undergraduate students as part of their studies, and the official word from BMW has always been 'no current plans'. So, while the possibility of a new Spitfire or TR cannot be completely ruled out, we can be reasonably confident that if the model name was ever to be revived, it would very likely not be powered by petrol and would lack the glorious sound of a Triumph exhaust note, the trademark of all Triumph sports cars.

Acknowledgements

Every attempt has been made to seek permission for copyright material used in this book. However, if we have inadvertently used copyright material without permission/acknowledgement we apologise and will make the necessary correction at the first opportunity.

Many of the photographs have been taken over several years and, in respecting the owners' privacy, I have erased vehicle registrations, except where explicit approval has been provided otherwise. Most images are my own, but some have been sourced from elsewhere, and these are clearly acknowledged within the captions.

I start by expressing my thanks to the many helpful Standard and Triumph car clubs, especially to the members who have willingly allowed me to photograph their cars and provide information and opinion on their cherished vehicles.

I must, as always, thank my wife, Ann, for her proofreading of the early drafts and final copy, indulging my interests with classic machines of all types and tolerating my sudden disappearances when an opportunity to gather some more photographs has occurred.